# Wild Goose Chase

## A Farce

## Derek Benfield

A SAMUEL FRENCH ACTING EDITION

SAMUEL FRENCH

FOUNDED 1830

SAMUELFRENCH.COM
SAMUELFRENCH-LONDON.CO.UK

## FOR PRODUCTION ENQUIRIES

### UNITED STATES AND CANADA
Info@SamuelFrench.com
1-866-598-8449

### UNITED KINGDOM AND EUROPE
Theatre@SamuelFrench-London.co.uk
020-7255-4302

Each title is subject to availability from Samuel French, depending upon country of performance. Please be aware that *WILD GOOSE CHASE* may not be licensed by Samuel French in your territory. Professional and amateur producers should contact the nearest Samuel French office or licensing partner to verify availability.

The first performance of *Wild Goose Chase* was given at the New Theatre, Hull, on 28th June, 1954, with the following cast of characters:—

| | |
|---|---|
| ADA .. .. .. .. .. .. .. | *Rosemary Davis* |
| LORD ELROOD .. .. .. .. .. | *Kenneth Keeling* |
| PATRICIA .. .. .. .. .. .. | *Pamela Jackson* |
| LADY ELROOD .. .. .. .. | *Doreen Andrew* |
| JENNY STEWART .. .. .. .. .. | *Susan Lyall-Grant* |
| MISS PARTRIDGE .. .. .. .. .. | *Eileen Essell* |
| CHESTER DREADNOUGHT .. .. .. .. | *Frederick Jaeger* |
| CAPONE .. .. .. .. .. .. | *Ward Williams* |
| WEDGWOOD .. .. .. .. .. | *Robert Chetwyn* |
| HILARY POND .. .. .. .. .. | *Brian Kent* |

Produced by FREDERICK JAEGER, *to whom the Author wishes to express thanks for his valued criticisms, suggestions and help in preparing this acting edition.*

The play was subsequently presented at the Embassy Theatre, London, on 24th October, 1954, when the cast was as follows:—

| | |
|---|---|
| ADA .. .. .. .. .. .. .. | *Virginia Hewett* |
| LORD ELROOD .. .. .. .. .. | *Gerald Welch* |
| PATRICIA .. .. .. .. .. .. | *Patricia Cutts* |
| LADY ELROOD .. .. .. .. .. | *Joan Haythorne* |
| JENNY STEWART .. .. .. .. .. | *Jean Burgess* |
| MISS PARTRIDGE .. .. .. .. .. | *Joan Sanderson* |
| CHESTER DREADNOUGHT .. .. .. .. | *Leslie Phillips* |
| CAPONE .. .. .. .. .. .. | *Tony Quinn* |
| WEDGWOOD .. .. .. .. .. | *Peter Bennett* |
| HILARY POND .. .. .. .. .. | *Derek Tansley* |

Produced by ANTHONY HAWTREY

---

*The scene throughout is the baronial hall of one of the last few remaining inhabited castles in England. It is the home of* LORD *and* LADY ELROOD, *two of the last few remaining pillars of the English aristocracy.*

ACT ONE
Morning on a day in summer.

ACT TWO
Afternoon, the same day.

ACT THREE
Evening, the same day.

*(No reference is intended, in this play, to any person alive or dead.)*

---

*The running time of this play, excluding intervals, is approximately one hour and fifty-five minutes.*

# WILD GOOSE CHASE

## ACT ONE

*The baronial hall of Elrood Castle. It is morning on a day in summer.*

*The scene throughout is the baronial hall of one of the last few remaining inhabited castles in England. Directly* U.C. *two steps lead up on to a rostrum which extends from* L. *to* R., *and from which two large studded double-doors, slightly* R. *of* C., *lead into a small outer hallway, and a flight of steps,* L. *of* C., *leads up and off to the* L. *A large mullioned window is* U.R.C. *at an angle of about thirty degrees, and underneath it is a large chest set about a foot away from the wall. A door* D.R. *leads down to the cellar, and another door* U.L. *leads to the dining-room, etc. Below this door* L. *is a table set against the wall. A large fireplace is* D.L., *with crossed halberds on the wall over it. On the rostrum and* R. *of the double doors is a suit of armour. A comfortable modern sofa is* L.C. *at a slight angle towards the* C., *and a matching armchair is* R.C., *also at a slight angle towards the* C. *A small table is set on the* L. *of the armchair, on which is a table lamp and a telephone. A standard lamp is in the corner* U.S. *of the door* L. *A hard chair is set* U.R.C. *against the rostrum, and another one above the door* D.R. *There is a bell-pull below the fireplace.*

*The modern furniture and colourful cushions and lampshades contrast sharply with the gaunt stone walls and mediaeval architecture of the castle.*

*When the curtain rises the stage is empty. Sunshine streams in through the mullioned windows.*

*After a moment one of the huge studded doors* U.C. *squeaks gradually open, and a mournful, bewildered little figure comes in. It is* ADA, *wearing a raincoat and a hat, and carrying a small travelling case. She blinks short-sightedly and comes* D.L.C. *gazing around in wonder. She stands still waiting for someone to appear, moves tentatively to the bell-pull, thinks better of it, changes her mind and gives it a good pull.*

*As if caused by the bell-pull, there is a loud report from off* D.R. *She jumps back to* L.C.

*Enter in a rush from* D.R., LORD ELROOD, *carrying an ancient shotgun. He is a fiery, war-horse of a man, with a bristling moustache and a twinkling eye. He rushes straight past her, up the stairs and off, breathing heavily.*

*She stands forlornly for a moment, and puts on her glasses, then*

*there is a second report from upstairs. She jumps.* ELROOD *returns from upstairs, still carrying the gun. He passes her, and then turns to her.*
ELROOD. That's that! (*To* C.) Haven't I seen you somewhere before?
ADA (*to him*). I was 'ere just now when you went through.
ELROOD. Oh, that was it! Never forget a face. Well, who are you?
ADA. I'm the new maid.
ELROOD. The new maid?
ADA. Yes, sir.
ELROOD. Well, if you go on wearing that hat, you'll be an *old* maid, as well! (*Laughs mercilessly.*)
ADA. Yes, sir. (*Forces a laugh also.*)
ELROOD (*suddenly fierce again*). What do you mean, "yes, sir"?
ADA. Well, I—
ELROOD. Do you mean yes, you will, or yes, you won't?
ADA. Yes, I will, sir.
ELROOD. Take it off, then. (*She does so.*) H'm. Better put it on again! (*She does so and he chuckles.*)
ADA. Are you Lord Elrood, sir?
ELROOD. Yes, I am.
        (ADA *notices that his gun is now pointing at her middle.*)
        What's the matter?
ADA. The matter?
ELROOD. You're shaking like a leaf.
ADA. Well, I'm a bit—
ELROOD. Frightened?
ADA. Yes.
ELROOD. Of me?
ADA. Yes.
ELROOD. Why?
ADA. Well—(*She puts her handbag between the gun and herself.*)
ELROOD. No need to be.
ADA. But those shots you fired just now—?
ELROOD. Oh, that! (*Comes closer to her, looks around suspiciously. Then:*)
        That's something I'd better warn you about.
ADA. Warn me about?
ELROOD. Yes. Did you notice anyone prowling around as you came in?
ADA. Oh, no, sir!
ELROOD. Well, he was out there.

ADA. He was?

ELROOD. Oh, yes! He comes every day.

ADA. He does?

ELROOD. Oh, yes! But he doesn't catch *me* napping! Thinks he'll fool me by dressing up in a uniform. But I know an enemy spy when I see one!

ADA. A spy, sir?

ELROOD. Well, of course! But don't worry—*I'm* always ready for him. (*Taps his gun reassuringly and moves* R. *He stops there, turns and comes back.*) By the way, how did *you* get in?

ADA. Oh, the door was open, sir.

ELROOD. What about the moat?

ADA. The moat?

ELROOD. Yes. You couldn't have used the drawbridge. It's never lowered without my orders. Can't think how you made it.

ADA. Oh, I—I managed . . .

ELROOD. Well done! (*Shakes her by the hand, vigorously.*) You'd better go and change your things. You must be soaking.

ADA. H'm?

ELROOD. And don't do it again.

ADA. Do what, sir?

ELROOD. Swim across the moat!

ADA. But I—

ELROOD. Catch your death of cold. Next time, give the signal like this —Ooo-oh! Ooo-oh! and I'll have Marcellus lower the bridge for you.

ADA. Thank you, sir. I'll remember.

ELROOD. Good!

ADA. Who's—Marcellus?

ELROOD. You must get to know Marcellus. He's the Captain of the Guard.

ADA. The Guard?

ELROOD. You don't think I live in this castle unprotected, do you?
    (*Enter* PATRICIA, U.L. *carrying some flowers. She is in her early twenties, and very pretty.*)

PATRICIA. Oh, there you are, Daddy. I've been looking for you. The postman says if you shoot at him just once more you'll have to collect your own letters in future. (*To* ADA.) Hullo. Who are you? (*She puts the flowers in vase on table* L.)

ADA. I'm the new maid.
PATRICIA. Good. We wondered when you'd be arriving. (ELROOD *makes for the stairs.*) Where are you going, Daddy?
ELROOD (*going upstairs*). To find Marcellus. Want to put him in the picture about this girl. (*To* ADA.) Remember the signal, now!
ADA. I will, sir.
ELROOD. Ooo-oh! Ooo-oh!
        (PATRICIA *signals to her to humour him.*)
ADA (*half-heartedly*). Ooo-oh . . . Ooo-oh . . .
ELROOD. Splendid! (*He goes off upstairs.*)
PATRICIA (*arranging flowers in vase*). Don't be put off by my father. He's really very sweet. He's just got hold of the wrong ends of too many sticks, if you know what I mean.
ADA. Well, I—
PATRICIA. Did he tell you about the drawbridge?
ADA. Yes.
PATRICIA. And the moat?
ADA. Yes.
PATRICIA. Well, humour him. He can't bear the idea that he's living in a castle that hasn't got either. It makes him happy to imagine them, and it keeps him out of mischief.
ADA. And—no Marcellus?
PATRICIA. No Marcellus.
ADA. Oh, I see.
PATRICIA (*sits sofa*). Now, I do hope you're going to be happy here.
ADA (*moving to* D.C.). I'm sure I will be, miss— (*Stops when she hears* ELROOD's *voice.*)
ELROOD (*off*). Marcellus! You blundering idiot!
ADA. —When I get used to it.
PATRICIA. It isn't always like this, you know.
ADA. Oh?
PATRICIA. In fact, I don't expect you'll see very much of us all. Mummy doesn't usually move from her bed until lunch-time, and my father's mostly on the battlements waiting for the postman.
ADA. Oh, I see.
PATRICIA. Apart from that, there's only my cousin Jenny. She came down from Glasgow to stay with us for Christmas.
ADA. Christmas?
PATRICIA. Yes—she's been here ever since!

ADA. Oh.

(ADA *picks up her case,* U.C. *Enter* LADY ELROOD, *from upstairs. She is wearing a house-coat and a slightly vague air.*)

LADY ELROOD. Why is there so much noise? It's still the middle of the night.

PATRICIA (*to fireplace for cigarette*). Mummy, it's almost twelve-thirty!

LADY ELROOD. Really? Oh, well, it *seems* like the middle of the night. Your father's been charging up and down like an angry bison all the morning. (*Crosses to vase on table* L., *passing* ADA.) Excuse me. (*To* PATRICIA *again*.) Whatever's the matter with him? (*Picks up vase.*)

PATRICIA. I expect he's bored.

LADY ELROOD. Well, couldn't he clean the car, or something?

PATRICIA. We haven't *got* a car.

LADY ELROOD. Haven't we? Well, we haven't got a moat, but that doesn't stop him shouting about drawbridges and things, does it? (*Takes vase to table* R., *passing* ADA.) Excuse me. (*To* PATRICIA.) Pity he isn't musical. He might tune the piano. Heaven knows it needs it. I *must* get someone to come and see to it.

PATRICIA. I don't see that it matters.

LADY ELROOD. Of course it matters, l·at.

PATRICIA. Why? None of us can play.

LADY ELROOD. It's high time we learnt. It can't be very difficult. I mean, you don't have to blow, or anything, do you? It's probably very relaxing. (*Carries vase to table* L., *passing* ADA.) Excuse me. (*To* PATRICIA.) Who *is* that person?

PATRICIA. She's the new maid.

LADY ELROOD. Well, why ever didn't.you say so?

PATRICIA. You hardly gave me the chance.

LADY ELROOD (*to* ADA). So you're the new maid?

ADA. Yes, ma'am.

LADY ELROOD (*to* PATRICIA). Isn't that nice? (*To* ADA.) I'm *so* glad you could come. I do hope you'll be happy here.

ADA (*apprehensively*). I'm sure I shall, ma'am.

LADY ELROOD (*doubtfully*). Yes . . . Well, anyhow, try and stay as long as you *can,* won't you?

PATRICIA. Mother! (*To* ADA.) You'd better go down and find cook, now. She'll explain your duties.

ADA. Yes, miss. (*Moves to door* C., *up steps.*)

LADY ELROOD. By the way, what's your name?

ADA. Ada.

LADY ELROOD. Oh. Well, *we* shall probably call you Millicent.

ADA (*gratefully*). Oh, thank you, ma'am! (*Open door* C.)

LADY ELROOD. And you won't wear that hat *all* the time, will you?

ADA. Oh, *no* ma'am! Only in the summer. (*Exit through door* C.)
     (LADY ElROOD *to table* R., *to pick up letter.*)

PATRICIA. Really, Mother, how do you expect us to keep a maid for more than a couple of days, if you talk to her like that?

LADY ELROOD. I thought I was perfectly charming! (*Sits sofa*, R. *end, and opens letter.*)

PATRICIA. If we all behaved a bit better, we might not keep losing them all the time. It's getting more and more difficult every day to get someone to come here.

LADY ELROOD. Yes. Nobody seems to *want* to work in castles, nowadays.

PATRICIA (*moving below sofa to* U.C.). I don't blame them . . . Why *we* go on living here, I can't imagine. We ought to sell the place, and buy a nice sensible flat in Earl's Court.

LADY ELROOD. Darling, what a terrible thing to say!

PATRICIA. It would be much better than staying on here.

LADY ELROOD. Good heavens!

PATRICIA. What is it?

LADY ELROOD. He's coming!

PATRICIA. Who is?

LADY ELROOD. Someone called Roger Newton-Strangeways.

PATRICIA. Who on earth is he?

LADY ELROOD. I haven't the remotest idea!

PATRICIA. Well, what does it say? (*To* R. *of sofa.*)

LADY ELROOD. It's from your Aunt Matilda. She says "How kind of you to let Roger come to stay with you for a few days". *Did* we say that Roger could stay for a few days?

PATRICIA (*crossing below sofa*). I shouldn't think so. Particularly as we've never even heard of him.

LADY ELROOD. Just a minute, though!—Yes!—Yes, I've *heard* of him —vaguely. I believe she did mention in her last letter how nice it would be if we could meet him. But I didn't reply.

PATRICIA. Are you *sure* of that?

LADY ELROOD. Of course I am. I never do.

PATRICIA. Well, *somebody* did.

LADY ELROOD. Why?
PATRICIA (*sitting sofa,* L. *end*). Mother—he's coming!
LADY ELROOD. We must stop him!
PATRICIA. We can't do that. I expect you did reply and you've forgotten all about it!
LADY ELROOD. Oh, dear! Whatever shall we do?
    (*Enter* JENNY STEWART *downstairs. A bright, pretty young Scot of about seventeen, she is holding a copy of the works of Shakespeare, and is quoting boisterously. She wears bright slacks and an American style shirt. Her hair is tied in two bunches.*)
JENNY (U.C.). "Romeo, Romeo, wherefore art thou Romeo?"
LADY ELROOD. Oh, Jenny, for heaven's sake! Couldn't you quote something else?
JENNY. Why should I?
LADY ELROOD. Because who ever heard of a Scottish Juliet?
JENNY. It's the feeling that counts, Lady Elrood.
LADY ELROOD. Feeling fiddlesticks!
JENNY. You obviously don't know what love is—*you've* never experienced it! (*To* C.)
LADY ELROOD. Oh, I see.
PATRICIA. I don't know what you see in him, anyway.
JENNY. I couldn't expect *you* to understand. (*Rapturously.*) To me—he's a young god!
LADY ELROOD. Who is, dear?
JENNY. Why, Hilary, of course! (*Above armchair to window* R.)
LADY ELROOD. Oh, I see. (*To* PATRICIA.) Which one is Hilary?
PATRICIA. The policeman.
LADY ELROOD. Oh—the thin one!
PATRICIA. That's it.
LADY ELROOD. Always seems to turn up just in time for tea.
PATRICIA. He stands in the middle of the High Street, directing the traffic (*Looking at* JENNY.) and apparently looking like Apollo.
JENNY. You can sneer if you like—but one day I shall be proud of Hilary. (*To below armchair* R.)
LADY ELROOD. I've got enough on my mind as it is, at the moment, Jenny, without having to bother about you and a romantic constable.
JENNY. He isn't romantic.
PATRICIA. Isn't he?

JENNY. No. (*Ruefully.*) That's the trouble!
LADY ELROOD. You see, we've got a visitor coming.
JENNY. Oh—who? (*To* C.)
LADY ELROOD. Roger Newton-Strangeways.
JENNY. Never heard of him. (*Turns* U.S. *and continues reading softly.*)
LADY ELROOD. Neither have I, but he's coming anyway!
PATRICIA. When does it say he's arriving, Mother?
LADY ELROOD (*looks at letter*). Oh, the twenty-fourth.
PATRICIA. What is it today?
LADY ELROOD. I don't know.
PATRICIA (*rises*). Quickly—we must find out! Where's the morning paper? (*Looks in armchair and then on chest.*)

(LADY ELROOD *and* PATRICIA *rush about, searching for the paper.* JENNY *is intent on her Shakespeare, and continues reading to herself and gesturing broadly.*)

LADY ELROOD (*looking under cushions on sofa*). I can't find it!
JENNY. "Thou art thyself, though, not a Montague—"
PATRICIA. It must be here somewhere!
LADY ELROOD. It isn't, I tell you! (*Bumps into* JENNY U.C.) Jenny, for heaven's sake, don't just stand there—search!
JENNY. Perhaps I can ring up the police station and find out—
LADY ELROOD. No, you can't!
PATRICIA (D.R.). Haven't we got a calendar?
LADY ELROOD (*searching on table* L.). No. I didn't buy any this year. We usually get so many at Christmas.
PATRICIA. We didn't get any this year!
LADY ELROOD. I know—you can't rely on *anyone* these days!
JENNY. "Romeo, Romeo, wherefore art—"
LADY ELROOD (*crossing above sofa to* C.). Don't start all that again! (*To telephone.*) Couldn't we telephone "inquiries"?
PATRICIA. I don't think they *expect that* kind of inquiry.
LADY ELROOD. There's nothing *else* to do! (*Lifts receiver.*) Hullo— "inquiries", please. (*To* PATRICIA.) I expect he's already on his way. (*Into phone.*) What? . . . Oh. Well, you see, I don't want a number at all . . . No. No, I want a date . . . A *date* . . . How dare you!
PATRICIA (*to* R. *of armchair*). Just ask him what day it is!
JENNY. "A rose by any other name would smell—"

LADY ELROOD. Oh, do be quiet!

(JENNY *shrugs and goes off upstairs, muttering Shakespeare.*)

(*Into phone.*) No—no, I wasn't talking to you! . . . No, I was—

PATRICIA (*wearily*). Do let me speak to him.

LADY ELROOD. No, No! I can manage. (*Into phone.*) Look, all I want
to know is if you can tell me what day it is . . . Yes, today . . .
The day today! . . . What? . . . Oh, thank you. (*To* PATRICIA.)
It's Wednesday. (*Hangs up.*)

PATRICIA (*exasperated*). Mother, we *know* it's Wednesday! We want
to know *which* Wednesday!

LADY ELROOD (*picking up receiver again quickly*). Hullo, hullo! Oh,
you're still there! Which Wednesday? . . . Which Wednesday!
. . . Wednesday the what? . . . Oh, thank you. (*Hangs up.*) It's
the twenty-fourth.

PATRICIA. Oh, good.

(*They relax.* PATRICIA *sits* R. *arm of armchair.* LADY ELROOD
*to* C. *They react suddenly.*)

LADY ELROOD ⎱
PATRICIA ⎰ (*turning together*). The twenty-fourth!

LADY ELROOD. Oh, dear! He may be here any moment!

PATRICIA (*to* R. *of* LADY ELROOD). Doesn't it say what *time* he's arriving?

LADY ELROOD. I don't think so. (*Looks at letter.*) No. No, she says he'll
send a telegram.

PATRICIA. Oh, well, that's something. It means we've got a breathing
space, anyway. What else does she say about him?

LADY ELROOD (*reading slowly*). "Although he is a very sweet boy, there
are one or two things about him which I ought to explain." (*They
exchange a look.* LADY ELROOD *sits sofa,* R. *end.*) "For instance, he
occasionally suffers from the delusion that he is being pursued by
somebody who wants to kill him." Well!

PATRICIA (*sarcastically*). Oh, lovely!

LADY ELROOD. "Do try to humour him, and never question his story,
but pretend to believe it."

PATRICIA. Mother, you don't mean we're going to entertain a lunatic?

LADY ELROOD. He does sound rather strange. (*Brightly.*) I wonder how
he'll get on with your father . . . (*Glances towards stairs.*)

PATRICIA. We can't possibly have him here! (*To below armchair* R.)

LADY ELROOD. But Matilda says he's really very sweet.

PATRICIA (*dryly*). Yes—but what *else* does she say?

LADY ELROOD. Well, let me see . . . Ah, here we are! "Should he suddenly say that he isn't Roger N wton-Strangeways at all, please don't argue with him but accept it, as this is all part of his little trouble."

PATRICIA. He sounds ghastly! (*Sits armchair.*)

LADY ELROOD. Oh, dear, I do hope he isn't going to stay very long.

PATRICIA. So if he says he isn't Roger Newton-Strangeways at all, we say "No, of course not, you're Little Lord Fauntleroy!" If we're still sane in twenty-four hours, I shall be very surprised!

(*Enter ADA from* C.)

ADA. Excuse me, ma'am. Miss Partridge is 'ere.

LADY ELROOD. I've never heard of her.

ADA. Very good, ma'am. (*Without stopping, turns and makes straight for the door.*)

PATRICIA. Just a minute! (ADA *stops.*) Wasn't that the name of the woman from the Archaeological Society?

LADY ELROOD. What *are* you talking about?

PATRICIA. The woman we met who said she was studying fossilized remains, and was going to write a book about life at the time of the Norman Conquest.

LADY ELROOD. Oh, yes, I remember!

PATRICIA. Wasn't *her* name Partridge?

LADY ELROOD. I believe it was.

PATRICIA. You said she could come and stay for a few days to examine the Norman remains *here.*

LADY ELROOD. Yes, but I didn't expect her to take me seriously.

PATRICIA. Well, she has.

LADY ELROOD. What makes you think that?

PATRICIA (*patiently*). Mother, she's here!

LADY ELROOD. Oh, is she?

ADA. Shall I show 'er in, ma'am?

LADY ELROOD. Well, yes, of course, dear!

(ADA *exit* C.)

Now, where on earth are we going to put *her?*

PATRICIA. The little room in the West turret.

LADY ELROOD. I can't do that.

PATRICIA. Why not?

LADY ELROOD. I'm putting Roger in there. She'll have to go in the damp bedroom next to your father's.

(*Enter ADA* C.)

ADA. Miss Partridge!

(ADA *withdraws.* MISS PARTRIDGE *enters* C. *She is an eccentric woman in her early forties, laden with bags, a small mallet, a large magnifying glass, etc. She is gazing around her, rapturously.* PATRICIA *and* LADY ELROOD *rise.*)

MISS PARTRIDGE (U.C.). Lovely! Lovely! I can *feel* the atmosphere already! A veritable hive of antiquity!

LADY ELROOD. I'm so glad you could come, Miss Partridge. (*She comes forward to shake hands.*)

MISS PARTRIDGE (*ignoring her and walking past her to look at fireplace*). You couldn't have kept me away for long. There's magic in this building! I can feel it! I should have been *drawn* here inexorably, even if you hadn't invited me. Ah! (*She taps gently three times on the fireplace.*) You hear that?

PATRICIA. Yes.

MISS PARTRIDGE. Better than I anticipated!

(LADY ELROOD *is above the sofa.*)

PATRICIA (D.R.). Really?

MISS PARTRIDGE. It has the *ring* of the Middle Ages! (*She moves* C. *gazing upwards*). Can you feel it?

PATRICIA. Feel what?

MISS PARTRIDGE. The atmosphere!

PATRICIA. Well, I—

MISS PARTRIDGE. It lifts you up out of the present—and *plunges* you back into the past! Oh, if these walls could speak! (*Piles her things on to* PATRICIA.) Come—I mustn't waste a precious minute! (*To* U.C.)

LADY ELROOD (D.L. *of sofa*). Perhaps you'd show Miss Partridge to her room, Pat.

PATRICIA (*half-heartedly*). Yes, of course. (*Above armchair to stairs.*)

LADY ELROOD. I'm afraid it's not quite ready, yet, Miss Partridge, but we'll soon have it fixed up.

MISS PARTRIDGE. I shan't spend much time in slumber, I can promise you.

PATRICIA. This way, Miss Partridge. (*Exit upstairs.*)

MISS PARTRIDGE. Oh, thank you. Thank you! This is going to be fascinating work. The very rafters themselves are pregnant with a sense of the past! (*She goes off upstairs.*)

(LADY ELROOD *sighs. Enter* ADA, *without her glasses,* C.)

ADA. Cook says are you ready for lunch, ma'am?

LADY ELROOD (*to* L. *of* ADA, *on rostrum*). Ah! Emily! Tell her there'll be two extra for lunch. Miss Partridge has just arrived, and then there's a Mr. Roger Newton-Strangeways. He'll be here at any moment. Now, when he comes, he may behave in a rather strange manner.

ADA. Oh?

LADY ELROOD. If he does, you must try not to notice it. You see, he isn't very well.

ADA. Do you mean he's barmy?

LADY ELROOD. Er—no—not exactly, dear. A little—eccentric, shall we say?

ADA. Oh?

LADY ELROOD. So—be prepared! (*Exit upstairs.*)

ADA. Yes, ma'am . . .

    (*She turns to go and bumps into the suit of armour which stands* R. *of the door* C.)

Oh, I'm sorry, sir.

    (*Turns to go, comes back, puzzled. She gets out glasses and puts them on. She sees the suit of armour, reacts, giggles, and goes off* C.

    For a moment the stage is empty, then a young man appears cautiously through the open doorway* C. *He is carrying a camera on a tripod, and a small suitcase. His hat is on the back of his head. He is a trifle breathless. This is* CHESTER DREADNOUGHT.

    *He puts down his case* U.R.C., *and stands the camera* U.L. *of table* R. *He puts his hat on top of the camera, and wanders below armchair to* D.R., *gazing around. He crosses to below sofa, and then backs towards camera, looking* L. *He almost bangs into camera, looks round, sees his own hat and jumps with fright. While he is looking* R., ADA *enters* C. *and comes to his* L. *He jumps again.*)

Oh, there you are!

CHESTER. What? Oh, yes! So I am!

ADA. I was *looking* for someone.

CHESTER. Well, now you've *found* someone.

ADA. I'm not sure if you're the person they're expecting.

CHESTER. Oh, I see—they're expecting someone?

ADA. Why, yes, of course! Surely you know? Well, of course, you *must* do, if you're the person they're expecting, mustn't you?

CHESTER. Yes, rather! Of course I must! (*Glances towards window.*) *Who* are they expecting?

ADA. A gentleman called Roger Newton-Strangeways. They've never met him before, and they say he's a bit barmy!

CHESTER. So would you be with a name like that!

ADA. Are *you* Mr. Newton-Strangeways?

CHESTER. Me? No, of course not! (*With a sudden thought.*) Er—yes, —Yes! I *am* Mr. —er—?

CHESTER ⎫
　　　　⎬ (*together*). Newton-Strangeways.
ADA 　 ⎭

CHESTER. Excuse me. (*Takes out a tiny note-book and pencil and makes a note.*) What did you say my first name was?

ADA (*remembering* LADY ELROOD'S *warning*). Roger.

CHESTER. Oh, yes, of course! I've a terrible memory for faces. (*Writes in the note-book again. She tries to see what it is so he moves away slightly.*)

ADA. Does Lady Elrood know you're here?

CHESTER. Lady Elrood? Who's she?

ADA (*patting his shoulder kindly*). She's the person you've come to see.

CHESTER (*extricating himself*). Oh, yes! I didn't quite catch the name. (*Makes another note.*) Er—what about Lord—er—?

ADA. Oh, he's up there. (*Points solemnly to ceiling.*)

CHESTER. I'm sorry. I shouldn't have asked. (*Looks solemn.*)

ADA. No! I mean he's gone upstairs!

CHESTER. Oh! I thought you meant he was—(*Points to heaven and flaps arms as wings, etc.*)

ADA. You'll like 'im—he's barmy, too!

CHESTER. Really?

ADA. He certainly behaves rather strangely.

CHESTER. Excuse me. (*Writes in book again.*)

ADA (*crossing to* R. *to indicate his camera*). Who's this with you? I don't think they're expecting you to bring a friend.

(*Looking bus. at her and camera.*)

CHESTER. What? Oh, this! I say, shouldn't you be wearing glasses?

ADA. Oh, yes!

(*She puts on her glasses, sees the camera, giggles foolishly, then looks at him and screams.*)

CHESTER. It's not as bad as all that, surely? (*To* C.)

ADA. I *know* you!

CHESTER Well, don't say it like that. (*Reacts.*) You *know* me?

ADA. Yes.

CHESTER. Oh, my God!

ADA. You *aren't* Mr. Newton-Strangeways.

CHESTER. Yes, I am—

ADA. Your name's Chester Dreadnought. And this is your camera.

CHESTER. Whatever makes you say that?

ADA. Because I can *see* it's a camera.

CHESTER. I mean what makes you say that I'm Chester Dreadnought?

ADA. Because you did me and my mum.

CHESTER. I beg your pardon?

ADA. You did me and my mum last Thursday. (*To* c.)

CHESTER. I did?

ADA. At four o'clock in the afternoon.

CHESTER. What? At tea-time?

ADA. Right in the middle of the High Street!

CHESTER. Right in the— What are you talking about?

ADA. You're a photographer, aren't you?

CHESTER. Yes—yes, I am. Why?

ADA. Don't you remember? Last Thursday afternoon you took a photo of me and my mum standing on the corner of the High Street. Surely you remember my mum? She was wearing her aquamarine two-piece.

CHESTER. So she was! I remember now. I'd only been in the town two hours—and you were my first customers.

ADA. So you can't very well be Mr. Newton-Strangeways, can you?

CHESTER. No, I suppose not.

ADA. You 'aven't sent us the photos, yet, either.

CHESTER. Haven't I? Well, you haven't sent me the money, so we're quits. (*Glances furtively towards the window.*)

ADA. The way you behave, anyone would think you were being followed.

CHESTER. Would they? (*Laughing.*) Oh, really! (*He stops laughing abruptly.*) I am.

ADA. You are? Who by?

CHESTER. Oh, a couple of men. They want to see me—rather urgently.

ADA. What for?

CHESTER. I'm not *sure*, but I think they want to kill me.

ADA (*delighted*). Oh? May I watch?

CHESTER. Yes, if you like. (*Take.*) No, you may not! If I'm going to

be killed, it'll be in private! What do you think this is—the French
Revolution?

ADA. Oh, no, I—

CHESTER. All right—well, put away your knitting.

ADA. Why do these men want to kill you?

CHESTER. I haven't the foggiest notion!

ADA. Why don't you ask them?

CHESTER. They might have a very good reason! And, anyway, I'd
rather not get too near to them. They might shoot first and I
wouldn't be able to ask questions afterwards.

(*A loud report from upstairs.* CHESTER *dives for cover behind armchair* R. *After a while he waves handkerchief over the top, and then
appears cautiously.*)

ADA. Are you all right?

CHESTER. I'm not sure. (*Puts hand inside jacket for a moment and then
looks at it.*) What colour's blood?

ADA. Red.

CHESTER. Oh, well, I'm all right, then. What on earth was that?

ADA. Only Lord Elrood. Cook tells me he does it all the time.

CHESTER. What's he shooting at?

ADA. The postman, sir.

CHESTER. Oh, I see. What?

ADA (*regretfully*). He never seems to hit him.

CHESTER. Oh, what a shame! Well, never mind. I expect he will one
day.

(ADA *moves towards door* L. *We hear the doorbell.*)

ADA (*turning at door*). There!—you see, he's missed 'im again. (*She
goes off* U.L.)

(LORD ELROOD *rushes down the stairs and off* D.R. CHESTER
*reacts.* JENNY *rushes down the stairs and comes face to face with*
CHESTER, C.)

JENNY. Is he here?

CHESTER. No, he's just left. Who?

JENNY. Hilary. I heard a shot. I thought he might be arriving. Sometimes he shoots at *him.*

CHESTER. Oh, I see!

JENNY. Only by mistake, of course.

CHESTER. Of course! (*Take.*) Who is he *supposed* to shoot at?

JENNY (*casually*). Oh, the postman, of course! Did they not tell you?

CHESTER. They did say something about it. I thought they were joking. (*Forced laugh.*)

JENNY. I don't recognize your face. Who are you?

CHESTER. H'm? Me?

JENNY. Yes. You look too sane to be in *this* house.

CHESTER. Do I? (*Glances to door* D.R.) Oh, well, there's plenty of time!

JENNY. What's your name?

CHESTER. My name? (*Consults note-book.*) Roger.

JENNY. Isn't there any more to it?

CHESTER. Oh, yes, a—a double-barrelled thing—you wouldn't remember it!

JENNY. You're not the one they're expecting?

CHESTER. Er—yes, I am.

JENNY. Ooh! (*She rushes off upstairs again.*)

(ADA *re-enters with telegram from* U.L.)

CHESTER (*indicating stairs*). What was that?

ADA (C.). That's Jenny, sir.

CHESTER. What have you got there? (*To* C.)

ADA. It's a telegram, sir, for Lady Elrood.

CHESTER. Oh. (*Takes it from her.*) For Lady Elrood? I say, look, this has come unstuck!

ADA. So it 'as.

CHESTER. I—I don't suppose it's *very* private, do you?

ADA. I don't know, sir. I 'aven't read it yet.

CHESTER. H'm. It might say what time Mr. Newton-Whatsit is arriving. If you turned your back you needn't know anything about it.

(*He takes off her glasses and gives them to her.*)

Go and have a chat with my friend. (*Indicates camera and pushes her towards it.*)

ADA (*turning*). What does it say, sir?

CHESTER. He's not coming.

ADA. What?

CHESTER (*reading*). "Regret unavoidably detained. Must cancel visit. Roger." He's not coming! Oh, well, that's that.

ADA. Huh?

CHESTER. How would *you* feel if you were expecting someone to stay, and they didn't arrive?

ADA. Well, I—

CHESTER. You'd be *so* disappointed.

ADA. Yes, but—

CHESTER. And they would, as well! So—we mustn't disappoint them.

ADA. I don't understand.

CHESTER. I—am going to be Mr. Newton-Strangeways.

ADA (c.). You are?

CHESTER. Yes.

ADA. Oh, no!

CHESTER. Oh, yes! Don't you see, I've *got* to be? If I leave here now, those men will probably kill me. Now, you wouldn't like that to happen, would you?

(ADA *does not reply.*)

Well, *I* wouldn't, anyway! If I can lie low here until the coast is clear—or at least until it's dark—I'd have more chance of getting away.

ADA. What about the telegram, sir?

(*He carefully tears it up and gives her the pieces.*)

ADA. Oh, I'll 'ave to tell them. (*Crosses* CHESTER *to* U.L.)

CHESTER (*stopping her*). Why? You're not a Girl Guide, are you?

ADA. Well, I—

CHESTER. You wouldn't be *lying*, exactly.

ADA. Wouldn't I?

CHESTER. No. You just wouldn't be telling the truth.

ADA (*doubtfully*). Well . . .

(CHESTER *quickly goes to his case and starts to rummage in it.*)

CHESTER. Look—I think I've got those photographs of you and your mum in here.

ADA (*excited*). 'ave you, sir? 'ave you really? (*To* D.C., *putting on glasses.*)

CHESTER. I'm almost certain. Yes, here we are. (*He brings a handful of photos down to her and looks through them. She looks over his shoulder and utters a cry.*) Oh, I'm sorry! How did *that* get in here? (*Puts a photo in his pocket.*) Here, this is you. (*Hands her one.*)

ADA (*rapturously*). Oh . . . Oh, it's lovely!

CHESTER. Yes, isn't it? (*Looks over her shoulder, frowns, turns it up the other way. He breathes on her glasses and polishes them for her with his handkerchief. Then he adjusts her head and photograph in right position, etc.*)

ADA (*not so pleased with it the correct way up*). Oh . . . Oh, yes.

CHESTER. Here's another one. (*Gives her another.*)

ADA. So—artistic!

CHESTER. Yes, isn't it? The clever way I've got the saloon bar of the Crown and Anchor in the background. Do you think your mum will like it?

ADA. I'm sure she will. Don't you think it just *does* something for 'er aquamarine?

CHESTER. Yes. Not *enough*, but it *does* something!

ADA. 'ow much do I owe you? (*Returning photographs.*)

CHESTER. Well, er . . . Look, I've got an idea!

ADA. Oh?

CHESTER. Well—if you don't tell anyone that I'm not really Roger Newton-Strangeways, then—(*Grandly.*) I'll give you these photos for nothing!

ADA. You will?

CHESTER. Certainly!

ADA. Oh, thank you! Thank you, Mr. Newton-Strangeways!

(*Enter* LORD ELROOD *angrily* D.R., *carrying his gun. He sees* CHESTER.)

ELROOD. Aah! I've been looking for you, Marcellus!

CHESTER. What? (*Looks at* ADA.)

ADA (*whispers*). It's Lord Elrood.

CHESTER. Oh! (*To* LORD ELROOD.) We thought you were— (*Repeats heaven and wings bus.*)

ELROOD. Where the devil have you been? (*To* R. *of* CHESTER.)

CHESTER. H'm? Oh—right here. (*Backs above armchair to* U.R.)

ELROOD. Why aren't you up on the battlements, keeping an eye on the men? (*Following to above table* R.)

CHESTER. Well, actually, two of the men are keeping an eye on *me*! (*Glances out of window.*)

ELROOD. Unforgivable! Ought to be shot!

CHESTER. That seems to be *their* idea!

ELROOD. How do you expect the men to respect you, if you skulk down here out of the line of fire?

CHESTER. I'm sorry, sir.

ELROOD. What's your excuse, Marcellus?

CHESTER. My powder was damp.

ELROOD. I see. Well, that's different. Why didn't you say so in the first place? Eh? Why didn't you say so?

CHESTER. I only just thought of it.

ELROOD. What!!

CHESTER. I mean—I— (*Crosses to* D.R.)

ELROOD. You *were* in line for promotion, y'know. You may not get it now. (*Turns and sees* ADA.) Who are you? (*To* ADA *at* C.)

ADA. The new maid, sir.

ELROOD. Another one? We had a new maid only ten minutes ago.

ADA. Yes, sir. It was me.

ELROOD. *You?*

ADA. Yes, sir.

ELROOD. Nonsense!

ADA (*coming nearer*). Don't you remember my face, Lord Elrood?

CHESTER (*to* R. *of* ELROOD). *Remember* it! How could he *forget* it?

ELROOD (*turns*). You be quiet!!

CHESTER. Oh, what a rude Lord Elrood! (*Retreats to* R.)

ELROOD (*to* CHESTER, *their faces close*). I say! You're an impostor!

CHESTER. I beg your pardon?

ELROOD. An impostor!

CHESTER (*mopping his face with handkerchief*). Spray that again, will you?

ELROOD. You're not Marcellus!

CHESTER. No. I have to admit—I'm not.

ELROOD. Well, who the devil are you?

CHESTER. Who the devil am I? Well, I'm—I'm the General!

ELROOD (*impressed*). Oh! I beg your pardon, sir. I didn't expect you in mufti. (*Salutes, and* CHESTER *returns it.*) I must report this to my immediate superiors.

CHESTER. Yes, of course.

ELROOD. And then I'll turn out the guard.

CHESTER. What?

ELROOD. Turn out the guard.

CHESTER. Why? Aren't they any good?

ELROOD. May I fall out, sir?

CHESTER. Yes, rather—right out! (*Quietly.*) The farther the better.

(LORD ELROOD *salutes and goes off upstairs.*)

CHESTER (*to* U.C., *pleasantly*). He's mad! Do you know that? He's absolutely off his nut!

ADA (*glumly*). I expect we'll get used to 'im in time, sir. I'd better get back to the kitchen, now.

CHESTER. Yes, of course. Here—these are yours. (*He hands her the photos.*)

ADA. Thank you, sir.

CHESTER. Then it's a bargain?

ADA. *I* won't give you away, sir.

CHESTER. Good. You're a sport!

ADA. Oh, sir! (*Sways towards him.*)

CHESTER (*restraining her*). By the way, what's your name?

ADA. Ada, sir.

CHESTER. Well, Ada, don't be too far away in case I need you.

ADA. Very good, sir. (*Turns at door* U.L.) You see, my *mother* was called Ada, too, sir.

CHESTER. Oh, I *see!*

> (*She goes* U.L. *He looks puzzled, shrugs, and goes to the window and looks out. He comes* D.R. *of the armchair as* PATRICIA *comes down the stairs. As he turns* D.R., *they see each other. A pause.*)

PATRICIA (*quietly*). Hullo . . .

CHESTER. Hullo . . .

PATRICIA. We were expecting you.

CHESTER (*with a disarming smile*). I'm so glad!

PATRICIA. I'd better tell my mother that you're here. (*Turns as if to go.*)

CHESTER (*to* D.R.C.). Do you have to?

PATRICIA (*stopping*). Why not?

CHESTER. Let's not overcrowd the room.

> (*Pause.* PATRICIA *to* C.)

PATRICIA. We didn't know exactly what time you'd be arriving. Didn't you send a telegram, after all?

CHESTER. Oh, yes. I expect it got lost on the way.

PATRICIA. They're very unreliable at the post office here. I'll phone them later on and complain about it.

CHESTER. Oh, no! I wouldn't do that!

PATRICIA. Why not?

CHESTER. I expect they're busy. We don't want to upset them, do we? And, after all, I am *here*—that's all that matters, isn't it?

PATRICIA. Yes, of course! (*Pause.*) Won't you sit down?

CHESTER. Oh, thank you!

> (*They sit.* CHESTER *in armchair,* PATRICIA *on sofa. A pause. He takes a furtive look at his note-book.*)

PATRICIA. Isn't it strange that we've never met you before?

CHESTER. Yes. It is lucky—er—strange! Well, I mean—it would have spoilt this meeting, wouldn't it? First meetings are so pleasant, aren't they?

PATRICIA. I don't expect you really know who I am.

CHESTER. Well . . . well, no—I'm not *really* clear. (*Bus. with note-book.*)

PATRICIA. I'm Patricia. *You* can call me Pat.

CHESTER (*gazing at her*). I'm Roger. *You* can call me anything you like!

PATRICIA. Is everything all right at home?

CHESTER. Absolutely splendid, thank you! (*He runs his finger round the inside of his collar.*)

PATRICIA. How is Phoebe?

CHESTER (*looks at her without expression*). Phoebe?

PATRICIA. Yes. How is she?

CHESTER. Oh—oh, she's pretty well . . . considering.

PATRICIA. Considering what?

CHESTER. Well—considering all the various . . . considerations.

PATRICIA. Oh, good. I'm pleased.

CHESTER. Yes, it is grand, isn't it?

(*As she looks the other way he mops his brow with his tie.*)

PATRICIA. Is she eating all right?

CHESTER. Who?

PATRICIA. Phoebe.

CHESTER. Yes. I think so.

PATRICIA. Of course, she can't be getting any younger, can she?

CHESTER. No. As a matter of fact, lately she's been getting much . . . (*Lamely.*) older.

PATRICIA. Pity you couldn't bring her with you.

CHESTER. Yes. Still, I'll tell her all about you when I go back.

PATRICIA. You must be very proud of that horse.

CHESTER. Horse?

PATRICIA. Yes.

CHESTER (*starting to laugh*). Oh, I see!

PATRICIA. Whatever's the matter?

CHESTER. Oh, nothing! (*Laughs.*)

PATRICIA (*rising*). Are you all right?

CHESTER. Oh, yes—fine! (*Stops laughing gradually.*) I'm sorry. That was very rude of me.

(*Enter* LADY ELROOD, *from upstairs, wearing a summer dress.* CHESTER *and* PATRICIA *rise.*)

LADY ELROOD. Have you seen your father, Pat? Oh! I didn't know . . .

CHESTER (*gaily, to* R. *of armchair*). That's all right—come on in! Make yourself at home! (*Turns away and looks at note-book.*)

(PATRICIA *gestures to* LADY ELROOD *that this is the person they are expecting.*)

LADY ELROOD. Oh! (*Crosses to* CHESTER.) Well, hullo, Mr.—er— How do you do.

CHESTER. How do you do. (*They shake hands.*)

LADY ELROOD. I'm Lady Elrood. (CHESTER *puts away note-book.*) I'm afraid we didn't get the letter about you until this morning.

CHESTER. You didn't?

LADY ELROOD. The postman's very erratic, you know.

CHESTER. Is he really?

LADY ELROOD. Yes. My husband shoots at him.

CHESTER. Oh, I see!

LADY ELROOD. So he comes at a different time each day to try and fool him.

CHESTER. I think he's very wise.

LADY ELROOD. So we haven't had a great deal of time to prepare your room. I hope you won't be too uncomfortable. (*To* C.)

CHESTER. I'm sure I shan't be.

LADY ELROOD (*turns*). Good! (*Pause.*) You're not at all what I expected, you know.

CHESTER. No, I'm not, am I? What *did* you expect?

LADY ELROOD. Oh, someone very different. Do sit down.

CHESTER. Thanks.

(CHESTER *sits armchair,* LADY ELROOD *on* C. *of sofa,* PATRICIA *at* L. *end of sofa. The ladies exchange a look.*)

LADY ELROOD. How is Matilda?

CHESTER. Matilda? Oh, she's pretty well . . . considering.

LADY ELROOD. Considering what?

CHESTER. Well, it's her hocks.

LADY ELROOD (*surprised*). Her hocks?

CHESTER. Yes. They're stiff. Very stiff.

LADY ELROOD. She didn't mention that in her letter.

CHESTER (*realizing his mistake*). Oh!—Auntie! Oh, well, she's better now, anyway. (*He relapses into silence.*)

LADY ELROOD. I'm glad you got here all in one piece.

CHESTER. Yes, so am I!

LADY ELROOD. Have you met my husband?

CHESTER. Rather!

LADY ELROOD. Where is he now, do you know?

CHESTER. I think he's getting the men ready for my inspection. (*As they exchange a look.*) Well, that's what he said. You see, I told him I was the General.

LADY ELROOD. You mustn't take any notice of him. He just hasn't quite got over his second childhood.

CHESTER. Oh, is that what it is?

LADY ELROOD (*indicating his camera*). I see you're a photographer.

CHESTER. Yes. Didn't you know? I took it up some time ago. It's always been a yen of mine, but I could never afford it before.

PATRICIA. Oh? Why?

CHESTER. Not enough yen. (*Laughs. The ladies do not. His laugh fades.*)

LADY ELROOD. Couldn't you have sold one of your horses?

CHESTER. Horses? Oh, yes—but I—I don't like parting with them. Sentimental fool, aren't I? (*Bus. of arm slipping off chair.*)

LADY ELROOD (*rising to* C.). How many have you got, now?

CHESTER (*he looks at her blankly*). How many?

LADY ELROOD. Yes.

CHESTER. H'm. Now, let me see. (*Pause.*) I bet you can't *guess*!

LADY ELROOD. I'm afraid I can't.

CHESTER (*to* PATRICIA). How many would *you* say?

PATRICIA. Oh—about seven.

CHESTER. Seven? You don't know for certain?

LADY ELROOD. No, I don't.

CHESTER (*to* LADY ELROOD, *triumphantly*). Seven!

LADY ELROOD. What sort of pictures do you take? (*To* R. *of sofa.*)

CHESTER (*rising*). Oh, all kinds! People, countryside—anything! My special interest is in the antique—old houses, old shops, anything that's ancient and musty. Would you like me to take a picture of you? (*He moves to camera. Realizes what he has said.*) Oh, I'm terribly sorry! I didn't mean it like that!

LADY ELROOD. I don't think we want a picture, thank you.

(*Enter* ADA U.L., *signalling to* CHESTER. *She sees* LADY ELROOD *and* PATRICIA *and stops.*)

ADA. Cook says the lunch is getting cold.

LADY ELROOD. Oh, all right. (*Moving to the door.*) Now, come along. (PATRICIA *rises and moves* U.L.) Mrs. Bessington is really an excellent cook—nothing is too much trouble! (*She and* PATRICIA *reach the door.*) Roger!

CHESTER (*to* C.). H'm? Oh—I'll be right there— (ADA *has been making weird signs to him.*) You go ahead!

LADY ELROOD. Very well.

(*Exeunt* PATRICIA *and* LADY ELROOD, U.L.)

CHESTER. Well?

ADA. They're 'ere, sir!

CHESTER. Who are here?

ADA. There are two men outside, sir! (*Points to door* C.)

CHESTER. Oh, no! (*To window* R.)

ADA. I thought they might be the ones you said was following you.

CHESTER (*below armchair to* ADA *at* C.). Well, what were they like? Was one tall? Dressed in black with a white face?

ADA. Yes, I think 'e was.

CHESTER. And the other—was he a little fat man?

ADA. Yes!

CHESTER. In a loud suit?

ADA. Yes.

CHESTER. It's them! (*Crosses* R., *and then up above armchair to* C.)

ADA. What are you going to do, sir? (*To him.*)

CHESTER. I don't know!

(LADY ELROOD *returns.* ADA *scuttles off.*)

LADY ELROOD. Come along, Roger.

CHESTER. Just a moment, Lady Elrood. There's something I've got to tell you.

LADY ELROOD. Really?

CHESTER. Yes. Come and sit down for a minute, will you? (PATRICIA *enters* U.L.) You, as well, Miss Elrood, if you please!

(*The ladies sit on the sofa.* LADY ELROOD, R., PATRICIA, C.)

I'm afraid this is going to be a bit of a shock for you. (D.C.)

LADY ELROOD. It is?

CHESTER. Yes—you see—I am *not* Roger Newton-Strangeways.

(*The ladies exchange a look. This is what they have expected.*)

LADY ELROOD. No, of *course* you aren't, dear—we knew that.

CHESTER. You *knew*?

LADY ELROOD. Of course we did. (*To* PATRICIA.) How could he possibly be Roger?

PATRICIA. Absolutely *im*possible!

CHESTER. You think I'm making this up, don't you? I tell you, I am not Newton-Strangeways!

PATRICIA. Of course he isn't! He's the General.

CHESTER. I'm not the General, either!

LADY ELROOD. Lawrence of Arabia?

CHESTER. No! Look, for the last time, I am *not* the person you were expecting!

PATRICIA. What shall we call you now, then?

CHESTER. My name is Chester Dreadnought.

(*The ladies giggle together at what sounds like a monstrous fiction.*)

LADY ELROOD. Yes, all right. (*Giggles again.*)

CHESTER. I am in terrible danger!

PATRICIA (*calmly*). You are?

CHESTER. There are two men outside—and they're looking for *me*!

LADY ELROOD. Really?

CHESTER. If they find me, they'll kill me!

LADY ELROOD. Yes, dear, but do come and have some lunch first. (*Rising.*)

CHESTER (*putting her back on to sofa*). Look—will you please take me seriously for one second? I know you don't believe me—why, I can't imagine—but I came here under false pretences because I was running away from those two men! They're outside now! They'll get in here somehow, and when they do, they'll murder me!

PAT. What makes you think they want to murder you?

CHESTER. If you'd ever *seen* them, you'd understand! I tell you, they *look* like killers! For nearly a week now, they've been following me —wherever I go! (*He comes nearer.*) Look! Couldn't you hide me somewhere—just until the danger is past?

LADY ELROOD. Now, Roger, do you seriously imagine that two strange men are going to be permitted to walk into this room and start murdering people?

CHESTER. Well—aren't they?

LADY ELROOD. Of course not! If any strangers entered that door, I should order them off the premises.

CHESTER. You mean that?

LADY ELROOD. Of course I mean it.

CHESTER. Then you'd protect me?

LADY ELROOD. Certainly! I should send for the police.

CHESTER (*with relief*). May I call you Mother? (*Kneels at her feet.*)

    *But at that moment the door* C. *opens and the two men whom* CHESTER *has described walk in.* LADY ELROOD *and* PAT *are completely shattered. For a moment* CHESTER *is frozen to the spot, then he rushes madly across the stage and out through the door* D.R. PATRICIA *and* LADY ELROOD *still cannot believe their eyes as the two men move down* C., *preparing to follow* CHESTER. *With a cry,* LADY ELROOD *faints into* PATRICIA'S *arms as—*

THE CURTAIN FALLS.

# ACT TWO

*Afternoon of the same day.*

*When the curtain rises, the stage is empty. After a moment* ADA
*enters,* U.L., *carrying a duster. She looks around carefully, and then goes
to the telephone and dials a number, putting down the duster on back of
armchair.*

ADA. 'ullo! Is that you, Mum? This is me . . . Ada! . . . Oh,
I'm all right, but I don't like it 'ere. . . . No, I shall 'ave to leave.
I think they're all a bit barmy! (*Brightening.*) But, Mum, d'you
know what? That nice photographer man is 'ere! . . . The one that
took that picture of you and me the other day. And do you know
what, Mum? 'e's given me the photos! . . . Yes, for nothing! Isn't
that kind? Oh, Mum, your aquamarine 'asn't 'alf come out a treat!
. . . What? . . . Oh, I don't know. Nobody's seen 'im for about
an hour . . . Yes, Mr. Dreadnought . . . No, he seems to 'ave disappeared. They can't find 'im anywhere. Any'ow, Mum, I'll ring
you tomorrow . . . All right. G'bye, Mum! (*She hangs up.*)

(*She goes off,* C., *leaving the duster behind. When she has gone, the
suit of armour begins to move. It comes down the stairs to* L.C.

ADA *re-enters, picks up her duster, and then sees the armour. She
is about to scream. The figure in the suit of armour opens up the visor.
It is* CHESTER.)

CHESTER. Don't scream! (*She screams.*) It's only me!

ADA. Oh! Oh, sir!

CHESTER. Now relax—everything's all right.

ADA. I didn't recognize you, sir.

CHESTER. Well, I'm not surprised!

ADA. What are you doing in there, sir?

CHESTER. I'm hiding! What the hell do you *think* I'm doing?

ADA. Hiding?

CHESTER. Yes—from those two men.

ADA. Are they still 'ere, sir?

CHESTER. Yes, of course they're still here!

ADA. I thought they were going to kill you.

CHESTER. Well, don't sound so disappointed! There's plenty of time.
They haven't gone, yet. (*Bus. of walking, etc.*)

ADA. Why don't you sit down for a bit, sir?

CHESTER. Sit down? I don't know if I can.

(*Bus. of trying to sit. Eventually he succeeds. Sits R. end of sofa.* ADA *to L. of him.*)

That's better! I say, do you think this stuff is bullet-proof?

ADA. I expect we shall soon find out, sir.

CHESTER. Look, you're supposed to be on *my* side!

ADA. S'sh! Someone's coming!

CHESTER. Oh, no! (*Tries to get up.*) I can't get up!

ADA. You'll 'ave to, sir! (*Tries to help him up.*)

CHESTER. What do you mean I'll have to? I can't!

ADA. They're 'ere!

CHESTER. Oh, my god!

(*He pulls down the visor. She moves quickly to above sofa, and as* CAPONE *and* WEDGWOOD *come down the stairs, she starts to polish the suit of armour. Hold picture.* CAPONE *is wearing a black suit and speaks with a German accent.* WEDGWOOD *wears a loud check suit, and chews slowly. They come down* C., WEDGWOOD *on* CAPONE'S *R.*)

CAPONE. You are busy?

ADA (*in a strained voice*). The spring cleaning, sir!

CAPONE. But this is June.

ADA. Yes, sir.

CAPONE. Well, then?

ADA. Spring was a little late this year.

CAPONE. Have you seen Mr.—what was his name?

ADA. Newton-Strangeways?

CAPONE. Yes.

ADA. No! I 'aven't!

CAPONE. Well, keep your eyes peeled.

ADA. I will, sir.

(CAPONE *whispers to* WEDGWOOD, *and they go off upstairs.* ADA *taps on the armour.* CHESTER *opens the visor.*)

CHESTER. All clear?

ADA. I think so, sir.

CHESTER. Good—give me a cigarette.

(*She gets a cigarette from mantelpiece and lights it for him.*)

ADA. I think I'm beginning to be frightened, sir.

CHESTER. Yes. I know how you feel! Thanks. That's better!

(CAPONE *and* WEDGWOOD *are heard returning.* CHESTER *puts the*

*cigarette into* ADA's *hand and closes the visor as* CAPONE *and* WEDG-
WOOD *come down* C.)

CAPONE.  I just came back to tell you that should you—

(*He breaks off, as he now sees smoke coming out of the visor.*
ADA *also sees this, and deliberately takes a succession of quick puffs at
the cigarette and surrounds* CHESTER's *head with a cloud of smoke.*)

Do you always smoke when working?

ADA.  Oh, yes, sir!

CAPONE.  Most unusual . . . I came back to tell you that should you
happen to know where Mr. Newton-Strangeways has gone, there is
a small reward for information.

ADA.  'ow small?

CAPONE.  Five pounds.

ADA.  Oh, that *is* small!

CAPONE.  It could be more.  Think it over.

(*He whispers to* WEDGWOOD, *and they go off upstairs again.*
CHESTER *opens the visor, coughing.*)

CHESTER.  What are you trying to do—smoke me out?

ADA.  I'm sorry, sir.  (*Puts out the cigarette at fireplace.*)

CHESTER.  And why did you ask how much the reward was?

ADA.  I just wondered, that's all.

CHESTER.  Well, you just make sure that's all!  I can't stay in here a
moment longer!  Help me up!

(*She helps him to get up.*)

I'd better go this way.  (*Moving to door* D.R.)

ADA.  What's through there?

CHESTER.  There's a flight of steps leading down to the cellar.  You
stay here and cover up for me if anybody asks where I am.

ADA.  Very good, sir.  Be careful of the steps, sir.  (*Opens door for him.*)

CHESTER (*testily*).  Oh, all right!

(*He goes through the door* D.R.  *There is a loud clatter as he falls
down the steps.* ADA *giggles and shuts the door.*)

ADA.  Are you all right, sir?

CHESTER (*off*).  I'm not sure. I think my big end's gone!  (*Crash and a
yell from* CHESTER, *off.*)

ADA.  Have you got the helmet off, sir?

CHESTER.  Yes.  My head nearly went with it!

ADA (*hopefully*).  Shall I give you a 'and with the rest, sir?

CHESTER. No, it's all right, I can manage. (*More clanking, off.*) Ada! I *said* I could manage! You may shut the door.

ADA (*disappointed*). All right, sir.

CHESTER. Wait a minute! I'll tell you what you *can* do.

ADA. What's that, sir?

CHESTER. Fetch my coat and trousers. I left them in the next room.

ADA. Very good, sir. (*Exit* L.)

CHESTER. And hurry! If I have to start running again like this, I shall get nowhere!

ADA (*reappearing with coat and trousers*). Are these the ones, sir?

CHESTER (*coming in half-dressed*). Well, of course they are! (ADA *screams, averts her eyes. He takes his clothes and goes out* D.R. *again.*)

  (*As* ADA *moves towards* C., LADY ELROOD *comes downstairs, followed by* CAPONE *and* WEDGWOOD. *She comes to* C. CAPONE *and* WEDGWOOD *to above sofa.*)

LADY ELROOD. Come this way. The piano is through here. I can' think why you didn't say you were the piano-tuners in the first place. It really would have saved *so* much confusion. I do hope it won't take too long.

CAPONE. We will be as quick as possible. Our service is the best in the country.

LADY ELROOD. I think it must be. I wasn't going to telephone you till tomorrow! (*Sees* ADA.) Who are you?

ADA (*long-suffering*). I'm the new maid, ma'am.

LADY ELROOD. Oh, yes, so you are! (*Crosses her to sit armchair.*)

  (ADA *starts to go.*)

CAPONE (*to* ADA). You have finished cleaning the armour, then?

ADA. Oh—yes.

LADY ELROOD. Cleaning the armour? Whatever are you talking about?

CAPONE. When I came in here a moment ago, your maid was cleaning the suit of armour.

LADY ELROOD. Whatever for?

ADA. It was dirty, Lady Elrood.

LADY ELROOD. I see. (*Looks around.*) And where is it now?

ADA. H'm?

LADY ELROOD. Where have you put it?

ADA. I 'aven't put it anywhere!

LADY ELROOD (*rising*). Then where is it?

ADA (*backing* U.C.). I don't know! It must have been moved—but I didn't move it! Somebody's taken it! It's not my fault if somebody takes it!

LADY ELROOD. Now, look, I don't wish to—

ADA. If you think I'm a liar, that's fine! But if you're suggesting I'm a thief as well, then I'll leave first thing in the morning! What good would a suit of armour be to me, anyhow? I never took it, see? I never took it! (*Up the steps towards door* c.)

LADY ELROOD (*soothingly*). All right, all right, Angela— (*Following to* U.R.)

ADA (*fiercely*). Ada! I never took it!

LADY ELROOD. Er—Ada—all right, you didn't take it!

ADA. Well, I didn't! I never— (*To door* c.)

LADY ELROOD. All right. I believe you.

ADA. Good! (*She goes out noisily,* c., *slamming the door.*)

LADY ELROOD (*dropping down* R. *of armchair*). What an extraordinary girl! I wonder where she can have hidden it . . .

(*Enter* CHESTER *from cellar,* D.R. *He sees them, turns and starts to go straight out again.*)

Ah! There you are!

CHESTER. Oh! Oh-hullo!

LADY ELROOD. We wondered what had happened to you.

CHESTER. Oh, I got lost! Silly, wasn't it?

CAPONE. Lost? (*Moving* c., *followed by* WEDGWOOD.)

CHESTER. Yes—these old castles are very tricky places, you know. (*To* LADY ELROOD, D.R.) Lady Elrood, I wasn't lying, you see.

(CAPONE *whispers to* WEDGWOOD.)

LADY ELROOD. Lying, dear? What about?

CHESTER. Well, about the two men who were following me—*those* two men!

LADY ELROOD. These two gentlemen?

CHESTER. Yes.

LADY ELROOD. Don't be ridiculous, Roger! They weren't following you.

CHESTER. They weren't?

LADY ELROOD. No.

CHESTER. Then what are they doing here?

LADY ELROOD. They're the piano tuners.

CHESTER. Piano tuners?

LADY ELROOD. Certainly!

(*He looks at* CAPONE *and* WEDGWOOD, *then back to* LADY ELROOD.)

CHESTER. Are you sure?

LADY ELROOD. Positive!

CHESTER. Oh, well, that's all right, then!

LADY ELROOD. Well, I think I shall leave you to it. (*Turns to go up* C., *passing* CAPONE *and* WEDGWOOD *who are now* U.C.)

CHESTER. Oh! must you?

LADY ELROOD. I'd only be in the way if I remained.

(CHESTER *crosses to her at foot of stairs.* CAPONE *is* U.C., WEDGWOOD R. *of him.*)

CHESTER. No, you wouldn't! I'm sure these gentlemen would *like* you to stay. Wouldn't you? (*No reply.*) You see! they'd be delighted!

LADY ELROOD. You can go and give them a hand.

CHESTER. I think they want more than just my hand!

CAPONE. *We* would *like* you to come and help us. (*Fold his arms.*)

CHESTER. You would? Oh, well, that's different! Why didn't you say so? (*Pats* CAPONE *heartily, and feels the outline of a gun in his pocket. He rushes to* LADY ELROOD.) I'd rather go with you!

CAPONE (*sweetly*). We *insist* that you stay with us. (*The gun in his pocket points at* CHESTER, *unseen by* LADY ELROOD.)

CHESTER (*seeing the shape of the gun*). Oh—oh, very well. (*Reluctantly moves to* L. *of sofa.*)

LADY ELROOD. That's splendid! (*With a bright smile.*) Now, you can get on with the good work!

(CHESTER *looks at her quickly. She goes upstairs.* CHESTER *sits* C. *sofa.* CAPONE *and* WEDGWOOD *come to either side of him,* CAPONE R. *of sofa.* WEDGWOOD L.)

CHESTER. Close, isn't it? (*They move nearer.*) It's getting closer. Don't you just love this time of the year? H'm . . . Quite suddenly it's autumn. I can feel the sap running back into my roots.

CAPONE. Mr. Dreadnought—

CHESTER. You know my name?

CAPONE. Certainly.

CHESTER. But *I* don't know yours.

CAPONE. My name is Capone.

CHESTER. Capone? I say!—not—?

CAPONE. No.

CHESTER. Oh, what a shame!

CAPONE. And this is Mr. Wedgwood.

CHESTER. Wedgwood? I shall have to treat him very gently.

CAPONE. Mr. Dreadnought, I am a very patient man. And so is Mr. Wedgwood.

CHESTER. Really? Is he always as chatty as this?

CAPONE. Why don't you hand it over to us now, and save yourself any further . . . embarrassment?

CHESTER. Hand it over?

CAPONE. Yes.

CHESTER. What—now?

CAPONE. Yes.

CHESTER. I couldn't possibly!

CAPONE. Why not?

CHESTER. I don't know what it is.

CAPONE. Perhaps, Mr. Dreadnought, you have observed a little anxiety on the part of my friend and myself to secure something which you have in your possession? Now—where is it?

CHESTER. Let me see—where *is* it? Have you tried the—? No, it couldn't be there!

CAPONE (*loudly*). That is enough!

CHESTER (*hurt*). All right! No need to shout. Anyone would think I was deaf . . .

CAPONE (*moving C.*). We will give you a certain time in which to find it—

CHESTER. But I don't *know* what—!

CAPONE (*turns*). If in that time you have *not* found it, you know what will happen?

CHESTER. Er—can I have three guesses?

CAPONE. No!

CHESTER. Two . . .?

CAPONE. No!!

CHESTER. Well, you tell me. What will happen?

(*Facing out front, CAPONE makes three bloodcurdling gestures, with appropriate noises, to demonstrate cutting CHESTER from throat to stomach, pulling rib cage apart and extracting his heart.*)

I beg your pardon? (*CAPONE repeats bus.*) That's what I thought you said. You really ought to go and tune that piano, you know.

CAPONE. You be quiet!

CHESTER. There you go again. Only trying to help. Shan't bother in future . . . I might have been able to help you. I used to *be* a piano-tuner . . .

CAPONE. Why did you give it up?

CHESTER. I was too highly strung.

(*A shot from upstairs.* CAPONE *steps to* U.R.C., *looking upstairs,* WEDGWOOD *to his* L.)

CAPONE. What's that?

CHESTER (*rising*). It's all right. That'll be the postman.

CAPONE. The postman?

CHESTER. Yes. By the way, have you *met* Lord Elrood? (*To* U.C.)

CAPONE. No . . .

CHESTER. Well, here's your chance!

(LORD ELROOD *rushes downstairs, past them and off* D.R.) *That* was Lord Elrood.

CAPONE. But why does—?

CHESTER. S'sh! (*He listens attentively. There is a second report from off* D.R. *He is satisfied.*) You were saying? (*Moving* D.C.)

CAPONE. We are wasting time. (*To* R. *of* CHESTER. WEDGWOOD *to* L.) We will give you precisely ten seconds in which to find it.

CHESTER. Ten seconds?

CAPONE. Yes.

CHESTER. What time is it, now?

CAPONE (*looks at watch*). Five to four.

CHESTER. Five to four! Is it really? I didn't realize it was so late. Excuse me a moment! (*He goes to the telephone and lifts the receiver.*) Hullo . . . Is that you, Mother? I'm afraid I shan't be home for dinner tonight . . . No. Something unexpected has cropped up . . .

(CAPONE *moves behind* CHESTER *to above armchair.* WEDGWOOD *comes in* C.)

No, don't wait up. I may be very late. In fact, I may not be in at all. Goodbye, Mom! (*Hangs up.*)

(CAPONE *holds up the connecting plug, which he has pulled out of its socket.*)

CAPONE. This 'phone is not connected.

CHESTER. Oh, that's all right. My mum's at the pictures!

(*He dodges* CAPONE *and rushes off* D.R., *pursued by* CAPONE *and* WEDGWOOD.)

MISS PARTRIDGE *enters from* U.L., *and wanders across the stage to* D.C., *examining a piece of stone with her magnifying glass.*

CHESTER *re-appears from the cellar at speed, followed by* CAPONE *and* WEDGWOOD. *As they dash across, they use* MISS PARTRIDGE *as a pivot. She giggles joyously as she is spun around. They go off* U.L. LORD ELROOD *follows in a rush and goes off upstairs.*

MISS PARTRIDGE *goes rather unsteadily* U.S. *to the window, still intent on her stone.*

CHESTER *returns breathless, and sits sofa. He does not see* MISS PARTRIDGE. *She goes on to her knees and starts tapping the floor with her hammer. He reacts to the noise. She comes* D.S., *still tapping the floor and listening intently. He sees her approaching. She taps the floor near to him, then taps his knee. There is no reflex action. She passes him. He looks at his knee, grabs her arm and takes the hammer from her, taps his own knee. It jerks up. He is relieved, and returns the hammer to her.)*

CHESTER. For a moment I thought I was dead!

MISS PARTRIDGE (*still kneeling at* L. *end of sofa*). I didn't see you there.

CHESTER. Well, I *tried* not to notice *you*!

MISS PARTRIDGE (*rising*). I'm Miss Partridge.

CHESTER. Who?

MISS PARTRIDGE. Partridge! Partridge!

CHESTER. Oh! How do you do, Miss Partridge-Partridge.

MISS PARTRIDGE. Only one.

CHESTER. H'm?

MISS PARTRIDGE. One Partridge.

CHESTER. Oh—Miss One-Partridge?

MISS PARTRIDGE. No, no! You mustn't call me that.

CHESTER. Why not?

MISS PARTRIDGE. It isn't my name.

CHESTER. Isn't it?

MISS PARTRIDGE. No.

CHESTER. What *is* your name?

MISS PARTRIDGE. Partridge.

CHESTER. Oh, I see! Miss Partridge!

MISS PARTRIDGE. That's it!

CHESTER. I bet you're game for anything, aren't you? (*Rises, to* C.)

MISS PARTRIDGE. I'm looking for Norman relics.

CHESTER. Oh, yes? (*Looking about.*)

MISS PARTRIDGE (*to him*). Yes. You see, I examine antique remains. You've heard of the ruins that Cromwell knocked about a bit?

CHESTER. Yes. How do you do. (*Shakes her hand.*)

MISS PARTRIDGE. I must explain. You see, I don't think anyone has searched here before. Just fancy!—Norman relics lying here all these hundreds of years—waiting for *me*!

(CHESTER *considers this.*)

CHESTER. I bet he thinks you aren't coming!

MISS PARTRIDGE. I must get on with the good work. (*Goes* U.C.)

CHESTER. By all means!

MISS PARTRIDGE. There's no time like the present—for delving into the past!

(*She goes off upstairs. Enter* PATRICIA, U.L. *with a telegram. She is thoughtful. She comes* C., *and* CHESTER *hears her.*)

CHESTER. Huh! Oh, it's you!

PATRICIA (R. *of sofa*). Who did you *think* it was?

CHESTER. I thought it might be Mr. Capone.

PATRICIA. And why should you run away from him?

CHESTER (*to* PATRICIA). We're playing a little game, you see.

PATRICIA. You are? (*She conceals the telegram behind her back.*)

CHESTER. Yes.

PATRICIA. You mean a sort of hide and seek? (*Sits sofa,* L. *end.*)

CHESTER. Yes. Only this is a grown-up version.

PATRICIA. What happens to the winner?

CHESTER. It's not the winner I'm worried about! (*To sofa.*) Do you know something?

PATRICIA. What?

CHESTER. I don't like this game.

PATRICIA. Don't you?

CHESTER. No. I'd much rather stay here and—talk to you. (*Sits* R. *of her, on sofa.*)

PATRICIA. You would?

CHESTER. Yes. With you I can relax. So I can!

PATRICIA. I'm not arguing.

CHESTER. Don't you see what it means?

PATRICIA. No.

CHESTER. Listen—my mother told me something once—

PATRICIA. Oh, I *am* glad! (*Rises to mantelpiece, glancing down at telegram.*)

CHESTER. Please listen!

PATRICIA (*her back to* CHESTER). I'm listening.

CHESTER. She said that a man should never marry until he finds the girl with whom he can really relax and feel at ease.

PATRICIA. What about it?

CHESTER. Well—all my life I've spent sitting on the edges of chairs—but now—*here*—with *you*—I can relax!

PATRICIA (*turning*). If this is a proposal of marriage, don't you think *I* should be sitting down?

CHESTER. I'm so sorry! (*He jumps up and puts her in his place on the sofa, then kneels at her feet* R. *of her.*) Well—what do you say?

PATRICIA. You haven't asked me anything yet.

CHESTER. Do I have to?

PATRICIA. Well, of course.

CHESTER. But I thought you *knew*—

PATRICIA. Maybe I did. But I've got to be sure that I'm not just jumping to conclusions, haven't I?

CHESTER. Yes. I see what you mean. Well . . . Well—according to my *mother's* reckoning—I ought to marry you.

PATRICIA. I see. What about your own reckoning? Do *you* think you ought to marry me?

CHESTER. Yes, please.

PATRICIA. But we've only known each other a few hours.

CHESTER. I know—but I may not have very much time.

PATRICIA (*making up her mind*). Besides, I could never marry a man with a name like—Dreadnought.

(CHESTER *rises to* R. *of sofa.*)

CHESTER (*not looking at her*). Dreadnought?

PATRICIA. Yes.

CHESTER (*to her*). Oh, but I wasn't serious when I told you that, this morning. My name's Newton-Strangeways.

PATRICIA. Is it?

CHESTER. Yes. Isn't it?

PATRICIA. I don't think so.

CHESTER. What makes you say that?

PATRICIA. The post office here have brightened up their ideas a bit. In fact, they've become rather over-enthusiastic.

CHESTER. H'm?

PATRICIA. They sent a confirmation of the telegram that *should* have arrived this morning.

CHESTER. Oh, you're joking!

           (PATRICIA *shows the telegram.*)

Oh, you're not! Good heavens!

PATRICIA. What happened to the original copy, I wonder?

CHESTER. I wonder . . . (*She looks at him.*) Well. I don't know. (*Crossing behind sofa to* L.) Does—anyone else know, yet?

PATRICIA. Not yet.

CHESTER. Are you going to tell them?

PATRICIA. I shall have to.

CHESTER (*coming* D.L. *of sofa*). Why? Couldn't you forget all about it? Nobody but you knows, so—mislay it for twenty-four hours. Couldn't you?

PATRICIA. Why on earth should I?

CHESTER. That's a good question. Don't you see, if I leave here now, those two men will kill me!

PATRICIA. How do I know you haven't made your way in here under false pretences in order to steal something? After all, what do we know about you?

CHESTER. I can't explain it all now, but you must believe me. Will you?

PATRICIA. I shall have to think it over.

           (*Enter* JENNY *from upstairs, to* C. *She is reading Shakespeare aloud. She sees them.*)

JENNY. Oh! I didn't know there was anyone here. (*Turns to go.*)

PATRICIA. It's all right, Jenny. You don't have to go. (*Crosses to table* R. *and picks up a magazine.*)

           (JENNY *goes to chest, puts one knee on it and continues reading to herself.*)

CHESTER. Doesn't she?

PATRICIA. No, of course not.

CHESTER. Oh. Oh, well, in that case, I suppose *I'd* better. (*Below* R. *of sofa.*) Twenty-four hours? If you don't, tomorrow I may be sitting on a cloud, with wings and an out-of-tune harp. (*To above sofa, turns.*) Twenty-four hours! Oh, well—never mind . . . (*Moving to door* U.L., *bravely.*) Be seeing you—I expect . . . (*He hesitates in the doorway, hoping she will call him back. She does not. He shrugs unhappily and goes out* U.L.)

JENNY. I think he's mad!

PATRICIA. He certainly has a vivid imagination. But I think he's rather sweet. (*Puts down magazine and moves* C.)

JENNY (*to armchair*). You're not in love with him, are you?

PATRICIA. Of course not! (*Crosses below sofa.*) Why, I've only known him a few hours.

JENNY (*kneeling in armchair.*) What difference does that make? I knew a girl once who fell in love with a man when the wires got crossed in the middle of a trunk call. And he was miles away!

PATRICIA. She must have been very silly.

JENNY. Do you believe in love at first sight, Pat?

PATRICIA. Certainly not! (*To fireplace.*)

JENNY. You will!

PATRICIA. Don't be ridiculous! I couldn't possibly fall in love with a man like that! (*Turns away, then looks back again.*) Could I?

JENNY. Why not? *I* did!

PATRICIA. Oh, *you*!

JENNY. When I first saw Hilary I knew he was the one for me. He was standing with his back to me, directing the traffic, and I just knew I could never love anyone else. (*Wistfully.*) All those cars stopping and starting just when *he* said so! I've loved him ever since.

PATRICIA. You don't know what love is.

JENNY (*rising*). Oh, yes, I do! And *you've* got all the symptoms!

PATRICIA. No, I haven't!

JENNY (*to* C.). You're looking a little flushed—

PATRICIA. I am not! (*Turns away.*)

JENNY. And your eyes are very bright—

PATRICIA. Nothing of the sort!

JENNY (*below sofa*). And I can practically *hear* your heart beating!

PATRICIA. Nonsense! I'm just rather hot and uncomfortable.

JENNY. Yes! That's a symptom, too!

(PATRICIA *tears up the telegram deliberately and throws it into the fireplace.*)

What was that?

PATRICIA. Nothing.

JENNY. What *was* it?

PATRICIA (*turning to her*). Mind your own business.

(*Enter* ADA.)

ADA. There's a policeman at the door, miss.

JENNY. Oh, good!

PATRICIA. Oh, God!

ADA. Shall I show 'im in?

JENNY $\Big\}$ *(together)*. Yes!

PATRICIA No!

(JENNY *rushes to above armchair, facing door* C.)

ADA. Well?

PATRICIA. I suppose you'd better.

ADA *(calling through door)*. In 'ere!

(*Enter* HILARY POND, *a thin, gangling young man in the uniform of a police constable. He might be either a radio commentator or a Mayfair playboy. He carries a dead goose by the neck, and is wearing bicycle clips. Exit* ADA.)

HILARY (U.C.). I say, Pat, I do think your father ought to be more careful with that gun of his! Look what I found in the middle of the drive! That's the fourth this week! Next time, it *will* be the postman. Damn it all if he goes on like this, I shall be absolutely forced to make a report.

PATRICIA (D.C.). I'm so sorry, Constable Pond. It won't happen again.

HILARY *(down steps to* C.). I mean, you wouldn't want me to spoil my record, would you?

PATRICIA. What record?

HILARY. Five years in the Force and not a single arrest!

PATRICIA. Don't you want promotion? You'll never get it unless you have a few convictions to your credit.

HILARY. Really? Wondered why I'd never been taken off the beat. But I just can't bring myself to do it, somehow. I haven't the heart. But if this sort of thing goes on, I'm afraid I shall *have* to!

JENNY *(in to him)*. Am I invisible?

HILARY. By jove, no! Hullo. (*Goes to shake hands with her but the goose is in that hand.*) Oh. (*To* PATRICIA.) What shall I do with this?

JENNY. Why not stay here and have it for dinner?

PATRICIA. Jenny! (*To above sofa.*)

HILARY. I don't really think I could do that. Besides, I've go to be on duty in an hour.

JENNY. Where will that be?

HILARY. Usual place—bang in the middle of the High Street.

JENNY. Can I come and watch?

HILARY. Why?

JENNY *(looking up at him, adoringly)*. You look so—romantic!

HILARY. Oh, come off it, old thing.

JENNY. You look like a knight in shining armour.

HILARY. Can't help that—it's a very old uniform!

JENNY. You look divine!

PATRICIA. I think I'd better leave you two together. (*Starts to go towards the door* U.L.)

HILARY. Oh, no! For heaven's sake, what would my Chief Constable say?

JENNY. I love you!

HILARY. He would not!

JENNY. If only I thought you loved me, too—

PATRICIA. Jenny, for heaven's sake—(*Down to* L. *end of sofa.*)

JENNY. Isn't there some way in which you could show that my hopes aren't entirely in vain?

HILARY. Well . . . Have a goose! (*Thrusts the goose at her. She turns away to below armchair.* PATRICIA *sits* L. *arm of sofa.*)

   (*Enter* MISS PARTRIDGE. *They watch her. Engrossed, she comes to* C. *and reaches* HILARY. *She looks at his boots first, then up to his face.*)

MISS PARTRIDGE. Good heavens! A policeman!

HILARY. Oh—however did you guess?

MISS PARTRIDGE. Are you interested in antiques?

HILARY. I'm afraid not.

MISS PARTRIDGE. From what I have already discovered, one thing emerges beyond any shadow of doubt.

HILARY. What's that?

MISS PARTRIDGE. Cromwell has been here!

HILARY. He has?

MISS PARTRIDGE. I'm certain of it.

HILARY. Oh, good show!

MISS PARTRIDGE. Come! (*She takes his arm and leads him down to the fireplace.*) Listen to this! (*Taps twice with hammer on* U.S. *end of fireplace.*) You hear that?

HILARY. Yes.

MISS PARTRIDGE (*taps twice on* C. *of fireplace*). And that?

HILARY. Yes.

MISS PARTRIDGE (*taps twice* D.S. *of fireplace*). And that?

HILARY. Yes.

MISS PARTRIDGE. What do you notice?

HILARY. They're all the same.

MISS PARTRIDGE. Exactly! (*With a significant look she crosses to the door* D.R., *and turns.*) I'm going to the cellar, now!

HILARY. Oh, jolly good luck! (*In to* C.)

MISS PARTRIDGE (*turns*). Thank you! (*Sees the goose.*) Oh!—where did you find that?

HILARY. Oh—he was lying around.

MISS PARTRIDGE (*taking it*). He may have been preserved in vacuo hundreds of years! I mean, how are we to know?

HILARY (L. *of* MISS PARTRIDGE). Oh, I think I could tell all right! (*Sniffs.*) You can have him, if you like.

MISS PARTRIDGE. I can? I say! This is most kind of you—most kind! (*To door* D.R.) This may be one of the most astounding discoveries since the Piltdown Man! (*She goes off, radiant, carrying the goose.*)

HILARY (*turns and finds himself face to face with* JENNY, *who has moved down to his* L.). Oh, hullo!

JENNY. Did you come here to see *me*?

HILARY. Certainly not! (*Evades her and moves below armchair to* C.)

JENNY. What?

HILARY. I came on business, as a matter of fact.

JENNY (*sulkily*). What business?

HILARY. I almost forgot—(*Turns to* PATRICIA.) —I've got to warn you to keep your doors and windows tight shut.

PATRICIA. Why?

HILARY. We're looking for a couple of men who broke into a jeweller's shop about a week ago. We lost track of them at the time, but they were seen in this area by one of our chaps early today.

PATRICIA. Are they very dangerous?

HILARY. Well, as a matter of fact, they are. Pretty violent records, both of 'em.

JENNY. Are you in charge of the case?

HILARY. Oh, I say, come off it! In charge? Me? You should know better than that. (*To* PATRICIA.) If I caught 'em, I wouldn't *keep* 'em. It just goes against the grain, arresting chaps. I can't bring myself to do it, somehow.

PATRICIA. So back you go to directing traffic?

HILARY. That's it!

JENNY. I'm glad!

HILARY. Why?

JENNY.  Because you look beautiful!

HILARY.  Oh, go away!

(*Enter* ADA, *pushing a tea-trolley noisily.  She passes above the sofa, down* C. *below* HILARY *and* JENNY *to* R. *of armchair.  They watch her in amazement.* PATRICIA *rises to below* L. *end of sofa.* JENNY *and* HILARY *are now above* R. *end of sofa,* JENNY *on his* R.)

ADA (*angrily*).  Tea!

PATRICIA.  Is my mother coming down?

ADA.  I'm sure *I* wouldn't know!

PATRICIA.  Well, you might find her and tell her that tea's ready, will you?

ADA.  I *suppose* so!  (*Moves to steps* U.C.)

(LADY ELROOD *comes in from upstairs.  She is wearing an afternoon dress.*)

Oh, you're 'ere!

LADY ELROOD.  Did you want me, Millicent?

ADA ⎫
PATRICIA ⎭ (*together*).  Ada!

LADY ELROOD.  What is it, dear?

ADA.  Tea!  (*She slams out abruptly* C.)

LADY ELROOD (*coming* D.C.).  Really, that girl was so nice this morning.  I don't know what's come over her.

PATRICIA.  Yes.  She didn't seem the belligerent type.

LADY ELROOD.  Now, let's all sit down and have a quiet cup of tea, shall we?  (*Sits armchair.* PATRICIA *sits* C. *of sofa.*)  Oh, hullo, Hilary.  Have you arrested anyone, lately?

JENNY (*to* C. *angrily*).  Please don't make fun of Hilary in front of me!

LADY ELROOD.  I'm not making fun of him.  He's a policeman, isn't he?  I just thought he might have arrested *someone.*

JENNY.  Well, he hasn't and I'm proud of him!  (*Goes back to* R. *of* HILARY.)

LADY ELROOD.  Oh, well—never mind—keep trying, Hilary.  One day you'll bring it off.  Then we can all go and celebrate.  Do sit down, everyone.  (*Starts to pour tea.*)

(ADA *enters* C.)

ADA.  There's a Mrs. Gribble in the 'all.

LADY ELROOD.  Who?

ADA.  Mrs. Gribble.  Says she's been invited to tea.

LADY ELROOD.  Who by?

ADA. She's by 'erself. How many *more* do you want? (*She goes out again.*)

LADY ELROOD. Mrs. Gribble? *You* didn't invite her, did you, Pat?

PATRICIA. With a name like that? No fear!

LADY ELROOD. Who on earth can she be?

(*Enter* ADA.)

ADA. Mrs. Gribble! (*She withdraws.*)

(*Enter* CHESTER, *dressed as a woman. He is in heavy tweeds, walking shoes and a wide-brimmed felt hat. He plays the part very much in the "landed gentry" style, with plenty of good outdoor vigour.*

*The positions are now:* LADY ELROOD *in the armchair* R., PATRICIA *on sofa, and* JENNY *and* HILARY *above* R. *end of sofa.*)

CHESTER (*entering*). How do you do?

(*He shakes hands with* JENNY, *then with* LADY ELROOD. HILARY *moves in below* JENNY *and extends his hand to* CHESTER, *who hangs his handbag on it. He removes his gloves, and then takes the handbag back again.*)

(c.) I do hope I haven't come too early.

LADY ELROOD. Not at all. We were hoping you'd come about now.

CHESTER. Really? Oh, that's absolutely splendid of you to say so! I do hope you'll excuse these old togs, but I really haven't had a moment to change. I was out all the morning watching my chestnut mare.

LADY ELROOD. Watching who?

CHESTER. My chestnut mare! Poor Cassandra! The old girl's bruised her fetlock. But she was very brave!

LADY ELROOD. How admirable!

CHESTER. Yes—isn't it!

LADY ELROOD. Won't you sit down, Mrs. Gribble?

(CHESTER *looks around for a seat.* HILARY *brings down the hard chair from* U.R.C., *and places it* R. *of the sofa.*)

CHESTER. Thank you. (*Sits hard chair. He realizes his knees are apart and hastily puts them together.*)

LADY ELROOD. You'll find the sofa much more comfortable.

CHESTER. Shall I? (*Rises.* HILARY *replaces chair* U.R.C.) Oh, no, I mustn't take priority! After all, I'm used to the rugged outdoors. You mustn't pamper me! (*Goes to sit on the hard chair again, but as it is not in the same position, he sits on the floor with a bump.* LADY ELROOD *and* PATRICIA *rise.* HILARY *helps him from* R. *Waving a finger at* HILARY.) Naughty! Naughty!

HILARY. I say, I'm most awfully sorry—

CHESTER. Don't apologize, young man. (*Hits* HILARY *saucily with his handbag.*)

LADY ELROOD. Are you all right, Mrs. Gribble?

CHESTER. I think so. You don't do damage to an old war-horse like me very easily, y'know! (*Sits sofa,* R. *end.*)

(LADY ELROOD *sits armchair.* PATRICIA *sits sofa,* C.)

LADY ELROOD. I don't expect you know Mr. Pond, do you?

CHESTER. Oh, no, I don't think I do. Ah! how do you do, young man. (*Shakes his hand.*)

HILARY. How do you do, Mrs. Gribble.

LADY ELROOD. He's a policeman.

CHESTER. Oh, is *that* what he's all dressed up for?

LADY ELROOD. And that's Jenny Stewart. She's staying with us for Christmas.

CHESTER. Christmas?

(JENNY *to* R. *of* CHESTER *to shake hands.* HILARY R. *of* JENNY.)

JENNY. I'm awfully glad to know you, Mrs. Gribble. (*But she doesn't sound it.*)

CHESTER. Good heavens! a foreigner!

(JENNY *pulls* HILARY *across to the chest. They sit.*)

LADY ELROOD. Pat, of course, you already know. Don't you?

CHESTER. Of course! Hullo, Patricia! (*Kisses her cheek.*) Hullo, Patricia! (*Kiss.*) Hullo, *Patricia!* (*Kiss.*)

PATRICIA. How do you do. (*She moves a bit away from him along the sofa.*)

LADY ELROOD. What a very nice costume you're wearing, Mrs. Gribble.

CHESTER. Oh, do you like it? (*Moves nearer to* PATRICIA, *without looking in her direction.*) I feel it's the most suitable thing for the open air.

LADY ELROOD. As a matter of fact, I have one exactly like it.

CHESTER. You have?

LADY ELROOD. Oh, yes. It's upstairs now.

CHESTER. Are you sure? Nothing like the old tweed!

LADY ELROOD. Now, how do you like your tea, Mrs. Gribble?

CHESTER. As it comes—wet and warm! —wet and warm!

(LADY ELROOD *pours tea.*)

LADY ELROOD. Jenny!

(JENNY, *reluctantly leaves* HILARY *and goes to* R. *of tea-trolley. She collects a cup of tea and a basin of sugar and takes them to* CHESTER.)

CHESTER. Many's the time a cup of tea has saved my life at the crucial moment! (*Taking tea.*) Thank you. Thank you so much!

JENNY (*offering sugar basin*). Sugar?

CHESTER. Thank you. (*Takes a handful and puts it into his handbag.*) (JENNY *returns sugar to tea-trolley.*

CHESTER *smiles at everyone, stirs his tea quickly and noisily. They all look at him and he slows down to a more sedate stirring. Taps the spoon delicately on the edge of the cup and puts it into saucer. With little finger extended he lifts the cup and drinks noisily. They all react. Bus. ad lib.*)

LADY ELROOD. Would you care for a little more?

CHESTER. Oh, may I?

LADY ELROOD. Certainly.

CHESTER. I'd be delighted!

(JENNY *takes tea to* PATRICIA, *collects* CHESTER'S *cup and returns to the trolley.*)

(*To* LADY ELROOD.) Have you a good seat?

LADY ELROOD. I beg your pardon?

CHESTER. Have you a good seat?

LADY ELROOD. Well, I—

CHESTER. Aren't you a horsewoman?

LADY ELROOD. Er—no. I'm afraid not.

CHESTER. You should be! It's grand exercise! I always have a canter before breakfast. You should try it!

LADY ELROOD. I will . . .

(JENNY *hands* CHESTER *his replenished cup.*)

CHESTER. Thank you, my dear. You are kind.

JENNY. I know, but don't mention it.

(JENNY *holds the sugar basin out to* CHESTER. *He opens his bag and returns the sugar he took previously.* JENNY *returns sugar to trolley, and takes cup of tea to* HILARY.)

CHESTER (*to* LADY ELROOD). Come out with me, one morning! I'll soon find out what kind of a seat you've got.

LADY ELROOD. Would you like a piece of cake?

CHESTER. Oh, thank you. I'd love that.

LADY ELROOD. Jenny!

(JENNY, *having just returned to* HILARY, *stumps crossly back to the trolley beside* LADY ELROOD. LADY ELROOD *puts a slice of cake on to a plate, and* JENNY *takes it to* CHESTER.)

CHESTER (*eyeing it*). It looks very wholesome.

JENNY. Aye! We've had it a long time!

LADY ELROOD. Jenny! (JENNY *returns to her place beside* HILARY.)
(CHESTER *bus. with cake, attempting to balance cup and saucer on knee, etc. The cake is very hard and he has great difficulty in eating it. Bus. ad lib.*)
Don't you like the cake, Mrs. Gribble?

CHESTER (*after looking at her coldly*). I love it!

PATRICIA. Have some more.

CHESTER. No fear! No, thank you!

LADY ELROOD. Please do.

CHESTER. No, no! I must remember I'm a lady.
(*He suddenly starts to choke, and gets to his feet with violent gestures.* LADY ELROOD *and* PATRICIA *rise. With the cup and saucer in his* L. *hand, he coughs violently which causes the cup to jump from the saucer and sail through the air. He succeeds in catching it neatly in his* R. *hand, and makes for the stairs. Coughing and spluttering he goes off upstairs.*)

LADY ELROOD. What an extraordinary woman! I'd better go and see if she's all right.
(*She goes off upstairs.* PATRICIA *to above sofa, putting cup on table* L. HILARY *rises and puts his cup back on the trolley.*)

HILARY (*in to* U.C.). I shall have to be going, if you'll excuse me. Mustn't be late, you know. My chief would be livid!

JENNY (*rising to* U.R.C.). I'll come and see you out.

HILARY. It's all right—I know the way.

JENNY. I'll come all the same!

HILARY. Thank your mother for the tea, Pat.

PATRICIA. Not at all. I *expect* we shall see you again.

JENNY. Of course you will! He's going to marry me!

HILARY. What?

JENNY. You are!

HILARY. I am not! (*Moves to the door* C.)

JENNY. Well, *I'm* going to marry *you*, anyway, so you can do what you like!
(JENNY *and* HILARY *go out* C. HILARY *reappears at once.*)

HILARY. I say, I forgot my chapeau! (*Picks up his helmet. Turns in doorway.*) Oh, I am impossible! (*Exit.*)
(PATRICIA *wanders down* C., *thoughtfully. She glances towards*

*the stairs, picks up* CHESTER'S *handbag from the sofa and looks at it. She smiles knowingly, replaces the handbag and crosses to the fireplace to light a cigarette.*

*Enter* CHESTER *from upstairs.  He comes to* C., *but does not see* PATRICIA. *Bus. of arranging clothes, pulling up stockings, etc.  Then he sees her, and quickly pulls down his skirt.*)

CHESTER. Oh, there you are!

PATRICIA (*to below* L. *end of sofa*). Do you feel better now, Mrs.—er— what did you say your name was?

CHESTER (*puzzled by her tone*). Gribble.

PATRICIA. Oh, yes, of course—Gribble. Where's my mother?

CHESTER. Oh, she's lying down for a couple of minutes. Poor thing's feeling peeky—can't think why!

PATRICIA. I'm not really surprised. We've had a very trying day.

CHESTER. Really?

PATRICIA. Yes. We've had rather an unusual visitor. A Mr. Newton-Strangeways.

CHESTER. Not *Roger* Newton-Strangeways?

PATRICIA. Yes. Do you know him?

CHESTER. Rather!  Dear old Rodge-Podge!

PATRICIA. He's a friend of yours?

CHESTER. Oh, yes. We're *very* close.

PATRICIA. I see . . .

CHESTER. Didn't the silly young fool tell you I was coming?

PATRICIA. Well, not exactly—

CHESTER. Oh, dear!  I am sorry!  You must have been taken aback! (*Below armchair* R.) Why, I was talking to him only this afternoon.

PATRICIA. Oh—you were? (*To above* L. *end of sofa.*)

CHESTER. Er—yes. I met him in the hall—he was going up to change.

PATRICIA. Oh? (*With a glint in her eye.*) Into *what*, I wonder . . .?

CHESTER (*in to* R. *of sofa*). He was telling me about you.

PATRICIA. Oh?  And what did he say about me?

CHESTER (*facing out front*). Well, actually—I—I think he's rather keen on you.

PATRICIA. On me?

CHESTER. Yes.

PATRICIA. Good heavens . . . (*Moves away.*)

CHESTER. Does that surprise you?

PATRICIA. Of course!  It never *occurred* to me, even.

CHESTER (*sits sofa, R. end*). Tell me—what do *you* think about *him*? (PATRICIA *moves to above* C. *of sofa with a smile, then she pretends to be serious.*)

PATRICIA. He's very amusing.

CHESTER. Yes. Yes? Well—what *else*?

PATRICIA. Nothing else. Except that I think he's rather plain.

CHESTER. You do? Oh come! Surely not? I always thought him jolly fetching!

PATRICIA (*to* D.C.). Yes, but then you're rather biased—aren't you?

CHESTER. Well—a little, I admit.

PATRICIA. I mean, have you seen his nose?

CHESTER (*feels his nose surreptitiously as she moves towards armchair* R.). What about it?

PATRICIA. It's a very strange shape.

CHESTER. Oh, I wouldn't say that exactly—

PATRICIA. And his eyes!

CHESTER. What about his eyes?

PATRICIA. I'm sure he's got a squint. (*Sits armchair.*)

CHESTER (*rising, horrified*). A squint! Well, *I've* never noticed it.

(*Pause. He moves to* C.)

(*Quietly.*) So . . . so you don't . . . I mean, you don't . . . care for him at all?

PATRICIA (*with relish*). No. I'm afraid not.

CHESTER (*slightly* U.L. *of the armchair*). Perhaps if you got to know him better . . .?

PATRICIA (*facing front*). I don't think so. You see—I'm already in love with somebody else.

(*There is a pause.* CHESTER *straightens up. There is a moment of absolute silence.*)

CHESTER (*softly*). Oh. I see . . .

(*He moves away above sofa, a rather pathetic figure in comic dress.*)

PATRICIA (*still not looking at him*). You won't *tell* him, though, will you?

CHESTER. Oh, no—no—of course not. I shan't say a word . . . (*To* L. *end of sofa.*)

PATRICIA (*rising*). I think I'd better go and see how Mummy is feeling.

(*Enter* CAPONE *and* WEDGWOOD *from* U.L. *They come to* C.)

Ah! Mr. Capone, would you and Mr. Wedgwood look after Mrs. Gribble for a moment?

CAPONE (*reluctantly*). Well, —er— we—

PATRICIA. I shan't be very long. (*Crosses them to foot of stairs.*)

CAPONE. We were rather anxious to—to find something—

PATRICIA. You can find it later. I'm sure Mrs. Gribble would be delighted to have a little chat with you. (*Exit PATRICIA upstairs.*)

> (CHESTER *sits* C. *of sofa, and tries to look invisible.* CAPONE *and* WEDGWOOD *are annoyed at having to remain with* MRS. GRIBBLE.)

CAPONE. Lovely weather, Mrs. Gribble. (CHESTER *does not reply.*) Mrs. Gribble!

CHESTER (*cupping his ear*). H'm?

CAPONE. Lovely weather!!

CHESTER. No, thank you.

CAPONE (*to* WEDGWOOD). It's all right. She's as deaf as a post. (*No reaction from* WEDGWOOD, *so* CAPONE *whispers to him. He then nods stupidly.*) I wonder where he can be hiding. (*Above sofa to* L. *of it.*) I'll find him if I have to take this castle to pieces with my bare hands! And when I *do* find him, he'd better talk or— (*Noise and bus. as before.*)

> (CHESTER *emits a noise. They turn. He pretends to have hiccoughs. In deep thought* CAPONE *sits* L. *of* CHESTER *on sofa.* CHESTER *reacts.* WEDGWOOD *sits* R. *of* CHESTER. *He reacts again. Neither of them take any notice of him, they are facing away from him, thinking.*)

CAPONE. He's not in the cellar.

> (WEDGWOOD *shakes his head.* CHESTER *sees him, and follows suit.*)

Or the kitchen.

> (*Repeat bus.*)

Or the attic.

> (*Repeat bus.*)

CHESTER. Or in the dining-room. (*Shakes his head.*)

> (CAPONE *and* WEDGWOOD *both shake their heads, but do not react to the fact that* CHESTER *has spoken.*)

CAPONE. I looked in the bedroom.

> (WEDGWOOD *nods his head.* CHESTER *sees him, and follows suit.*)

And in the bathroom.

> (*Repeat bus.*)

CHESTER. And in the—?

> (CAPONE *and* WEDGWOOD *both nod their heads.*)

Oh, good!

> (CAPONE *and* WEDGWOOD *both turn and look at him.*)

CHESTER. Lovely weather!

CAPONE. I seem to remember your face.

CHESTER. Well, I've had it a long time!

CAPONE. Who *are* you, anyway?

CHESTER. H'm?

CAPONE (*louder*). Are you a relative?

CHESTER. Only in the wet weather.

CAPONE. I am looking for a man.

CHESTER. Aren't we all? (*Saucily pushes* WEDGWOOD.) Well, now, what is he like? Good-looking?

CAPONE. Yes.

CHESTER. Blue eyes?

CAPONE. Yes.

CHESTER. Fair hair?

CAPONE. Yes.

CHESTER. Grey suit?

CAPONE. Yes!

CHESTER. Blue tie?

CAPONE. Yes!

CHESTER. No, I haven't seen him.

(*They face away from him. He fans himself with his handbag. Cigarette bus. see Production Note on page 3), ending with* CAPONE *and* WEDGWOOD *recognizing* CHESTER. *From now until the end of the Act must be taken at great speed.*

CHESTER *vaults over the back of the sofa as they dive for him, and rushes off* U.L. CAPONE *and* WEDGWOOD *collapse on the sofa, right themselves, and rush off after* CHESTER.

CHESTER *runs on from* U.L. *He picks up the soda syphon from the table* L. *and hides above the door* U.L. CAPONE *rushes in from* U.L. *and off upstairs.* WEDGWOOD *follows him, and* CHESTER *goes to squirt him with the syphon, but is holding it the wrong way round and squirts it in his own face by mistake.* WEDGWOOD, *not having seen* CHESTER, *follows* CAPONE *off upstairs.* LORD ELROOD *appears from* D.R., *with his shotgun at the ready.*)

ELROOD. Who's there? Halt or I fire! Who are you?

CHESTER. Florence Nightingale! Sound the alarm!

ELROOD. The alarm!

(LORD ELROOD *goes back into the cellar* D.R., *and* CHESTER *runs off* U.L.

MISS PARTRIDGE *appears from* D.R., *spinning slightly, having apparently been swung round by* LORD ELROOD *on his way past her. She is carrying the goose, magnifying glass and a stone which she is examining. She comes to* C.

CHESTER *comes in from* U.L., *carrying his hat and wig.* MISS PARTRIDGE *does not hear him, and jumps with fright when he places the wig and the hat on her head.*)

CHESTER. There! Very becoming!

MISS PARTRIDGE (*pleased*). Really?

CHESTER. You look cold. Have this as well. (*Takes off his jacket and puts it over her shoulders.*) There! (*He rushes off* U.L. *again, carrying the goose.*)

(CAPONE *and* WEDGWOOD *come downstairs.*)

CAPONE (*seeing* MISS PARTRIDGE). There he is!

(*They descend upon* MISS PARTRIDGE *with force, and carry her, protesting, towards the cellar* D.R. CHESTER *runs in again from* U.L. *sees* CAPONE *and* WEDGWOOD *and lets out a cry. The crooks realize their mistake, drop* MISS PARTRIDGE, *and pursue* CHESTER *off through door* C.

LADY ELROOD *and* PATRICIA *come downstairs as* LORD ELROOD *runs in from* D.R. *He rushes across and off upstairs, shouting.*)

ELROOD. Marcellus! Sound the alarm! Sound the alarm!

(LADY ELROOD *and* PATRICIA *go to help* MISS PARTRIDGE. CHESTER *appears from* U.L. *as* CAPONE *and* WEDGWOOD *come in from* C. *He throws the goose to* CAPONE, *who catches it and throws it to* WEDGWOOD. CHESTER *runs off* D.R., *followed by* CAPONE. WEDGWOOD *gazes at the goose, dumbfounded, down* L.C. PATRICIA *and* LADY ELROOD *are trying to keep* MISS PARTRIDGE *upright, but she continually goes limp at the knees, as she babbles incoherently. From upstairs a trumpet blares out the alarm.*)

QUICK CURTAIN

# ACT THREE

*Evening, the same day.*
*When the curtain rises the stage is empty. The room is only dimly illuminated by the table lamp.*
JENNY *comes furtively down the stairs, and goes to the telephone.*

JENNY (*in a hushed whisper*). Hullo, is that the operator? . . . Will you get me the Police Station, please? . . . Thank you. (*Pause.*) Is that the Police Station? . . . I'm speaking from Elrood Castle. I want to report a murder . . . Yes, a murder! . . . Well, I thought you might do something about it . . . Oh. Oh, well, perhaps I could speak to the sergeant . . . Thanks. (*Pause.*) Is that you, Sergeant MacIntyre? . . . Oh, I'm fine! How are you? . . . Good. Well, I rang you because there's been a murder . Yes, here . . . About an hour ago! . . . That's right—just before dinner. Could you send somebody over right away? . . . Fine! Could it be—well, somebody special? It might be a tricky case . . . Well, actually, I hadn't *thought* of Constable Pond, but he'd do fine! . . . Thanks. Good-bye! (*Hangs up and hugs herself, delightedly.*)
(*Enter* PATRICIA U.L.)
PATRICIA. Whatever are you doing in the dark? (*Turns on the main lights.*)
JENNY. Oh—nothing.
PATRICIA. Have you seen Chester? (*To* L. *of* JENNY.)
JENNY. Who?
PATRICIA (*hastily*). Er—Roger.
JENNY. No, I haven't.
PATRICIA. I can't find him anywhere.
JENNY. What happened to Mrs. Gribble?
PATRICIA. She seems to have disappeared as well. *Everybody* seems to be vanishing. (*As* JENNY *goes towards stairs.*) You might have another look while you're upstairs.
JENNY. All right, but I shan't have long before he arrives.
PATRICIA. Before who arrives?
JENNY. Oh—nobody! (*Exit upstairs.*)
(*As* PATRICIA *is about to go, the lid of the oak chest opens and* CHESTER *partially emerges.*)

CHESTER. P'ssst!

(PATRICIA *jumps, and then sees him.*)

PATRICIA. Why do you keep hiding?

CHESTER. Because I'm too young to die, and too old to keep running.

PATRICIA (*to* R.C.). What have you got to be afraid of?

CHESTER. What have I got to be . . .? Well, you *saw* them chasing me!

PATRICIA. Yes, but what makes you think they're going to kill you?

CHESTER. Do piano-tuners *always* behave like that?

(MISS PARTRIDGE *comes wandering in from upstairs.* CHESTER *goes back into the chest and closes the lid.*)

MISS PARTRIDGE (*apprehensively*). Is everything all right?

PATRICIA. Oh, yes, Miss Partridge.

MISS PARTRIDGE. Good. (*As she turns we see that she has a large black eye. She comes down to* C.)

PATRICIA. Are you feeling any better, now?

MISS PARTRIDGE. Much better, thank you. It was all very exciting, wasn't it? I was almost carried away!

PATRICIA (*doubtfully*). Yes. So I noticed.

MISS PARTRIDGE. Do you know, sometimes I can't believe we're in the twentieth century.

PATRICIA. I know exactly how you feel!

(CHESTER *sneezes inside the chest.*)

MISS PARTRIDGE. Listen! You hear that?

PATRICIA. Er—no.

MISS PARTRIDGE. It was deafening!

PATRICIA. I can't hear anything.

(CHESTER *sneezes again.*)

MISS PARTRIDGE. There you are! Echoes—of the past! I can almost *feel* another presence in the room. (*Moves vaguely towards the chest.*)

PATRICIA (*catching her by the* L. *arm and pulling her to above sofa*). Miss Partridge, have you heard the echoes in the dining-room? They're very strong in the evening.

MISS PARTRIDGE. Really? Then we must investigate at once! (*She goes off* U.L. PATRICIA *is about to move* R. *when* MISS PARTRIDGE *reappears.*) Come along, my dear! (*She pulls* PATRICIA *off* U.L.)

(CAPONE *and* WEDGWOOD *come in* C., *looking about.* CAPONE *comes down* C., WEDGWOOD *above chest to window.* WEDGWOOD *gestures to* CAPONE, *who joins him at window. The lid of the chest opens slowly.* CHESTER *looks out; he cannot see the crooks; then he gets out cautiously and moves to* D.C. *He takes out a cigarette, and looks for a match in his pockets. The crooks have meantime moved silently to behind him.* CAPONE *proffers his lighter from behind* L. *of* CHESTER.)

CHESTER. Oh, thanks! (*Lights cigarette. Then reacts, and looks* R. *and comes face to face with* WEDGWOOD. *Reacts.*)

Oh . . .!

CAPONE. You are causing us a great deal of trouble, Mr. Dreadnought.

CHESTER. I am? Oh, good!

CAPONE. Why don't you sit down?

CHESTER. The sofa isn't very comfortable.

CAPONE. Wedgwood! Try the sofa!

(*There is no reaction from* WEDGWOOD. CHESTER *whispers to him.* WEDGWOOD *then tries the sofa by bouncing up and down on it,* R. *end.*)

Well?

(WEDGWOOD *shakes his head.*)

CHESTER (*to* CAPONE). You see!

CAPONE. Nonsense!

CHESTER. *You* try it!

CAPONE. Very well. (*He tries it.* L. *end. He is pleased.*) Not bad.

CHESTER. Really?

CAPONE (*smiling*). Not bad at all!

CHESTER. Are you sure?

(CHESTER *tries the sofa also* C. WEDGWOOD *joins them, and all three bounce on the sofa.*)

CAPONE (*suddenly grim*). Stop!

(*They all stop.* CAPONE *to fireplace.* WEDGWOOD *to* D.C. *He has stopped chewing.*)

CAPONE. Now, Mr. Dreadnought, we are wasting time. Once and for all—where is it?

CHESTER (*rising desperately*). Look, you must believe me—I really haven't the faintest idea what it is you're looking for!

CAPONE. You do not remember?

CHESTER. Not a thing!

CAPONE. Then we will tell you.

CHESTER. Oh, thanks very much!

CAPONE. You are a photographer?

CHESTER. Yes.

CAPONE. You take photographs in the street?

CHESTER. Yes.

CAPONE. You were taking pictures in the streets a week ago?

CHESTER. I expect so.

CAPONE. You took a picture of a young man with his girl friend outside a shop?

CHESTER. I believe I did!

CAPONE. You do not remember what sort of a shop?

CHESTER. What *sort* of a shop?

CAPONE. Yes.

CHESTER. No.

CAPONE. Think!

CHESTER. Well, I— (*To* WEDGWOOD.) It's all right, you can stand at ease.

(WEDGWOOD *starts to chew again, and gives to* D.R.C.)

CAPONE. It was a jeweller's shop!

CHESTER. Oh, was it?

CAPONE. Now—in the photograph you took were Mr. Wedgwood and myself.

CHESTER. What? *You* weren't the young man and his—?

CAPONE. No!! We were in the background—coming out of the shop.

CHESTER. Oh, I see! And you want a copy? I never sent you the proof! (*In towards* WEDGWOOD. CAPONE *closes to* L. *of* CHESTER.) Oh, I am sorry. I get so forgetful sometimes! I expect I've got it here somewhere. (*Rummages in pockets and finds photographs. He holds one up. They all peer at it.*) No, that's not it! (WEDGWOOD *takes it.* CHESTER *slaps his hand and takes it back.*) You know, there was no need to go to all that fuss just because of a photograph. You'd have got it in the long run. Anyone would think you didn't trust me. Just a minute, though!

CAPONE. What is it?

CHESTER. I don't remember you paying me.

CAPONE. We didn't. (*Away slightly.*)

CHESTER. You didn't?

CAPONE. No.

CHESTER. Well, I shan't bother to look then. (CAPONE *turns and advances.*) It's no bother! What sort of a pose was it?

CAPONE. H'm?

CHESTER.   What were you *doing* coming out of the jeweller's?
(*Realizes.*) Oh! Oh, I see.

CAPONE.   Where is it?

CHESTER.   I—I don't know— (*Backs towards* WEDGWOOD.  CAPONE *follows up.*)

CAPONE.   You had better find it.  We wouldn't like that picture to get into the wrong hands.

CHESTER.   No—I—I don't expect you would—

CAPONE.   Because if it *did*, then *you* would be to blame.  And if you were to blame, you know what will happen.

CHESTER.   Yes!  I know!  (*They both do the bus. and noises in complete unison.*)

CAPONE.   So please—for your own sake—try to remember.
(*Enter* PATRICIA, *from* U.L.)

PATRICIA.   I thought you were tuning the piano.

CAPONE.   We were, but—

PATRICIA.   Then get on with it!

CAPONE.   Yes—of course.
(*He and* WEDGWOOD *go out* U.L., *very reluctantly.*)

CHESTER (*in to* U.C.).   You were just in time!

PATRICIA (*to him*).   Why?  What happened?

CHESTER.   Oh, we talked business.

PATRICIA.   Serious business?

CHESTER.   Deadly serious!

PATRICIA.   And did you find out what it is they're after?

CHESTER.   Yes.

PATRICIA.   What?

CHESTER.   My blood.

PATRICIA.   Apart from that.

CHESTER.   They want a photograph I've got.

PATRICIA.   A what?

CHESTER.   A photograph of them—

PATRICIA.   Do you expect me to believe that?

CHESTER.   It's true!
(*Re-enter* CAPONE U.L.)
Oh he's here again!
(CAPONE *circles round above* PATRICIA *to her* R.  CHESTER *circles below her to her* L.)

CAPONE (*sweetly*).   Hullo . . .

CHESTER. Goodbye!

    (*He rushes off,* U.L., *pursued by* CAPONE. PATRICIA *looks non-plussed. Enter* ADA, C.)

ADA. That copper's 'ere again!

PATRICIA. Oh, what on earth does he want this time?

ADA. I didn't ask him! (*Exit.*)

    (JENNY *charges down the stairs.*)

JENNY. It's Hilary! He's here! He's here! I just knew that he'd come!

    (*She arranges herself full-length on the sofa. Enter* HILARY, *breathless, with bicycle clips. He does not see* JENNY.)

PATRICIA (*above* R. *end of sofa*). Hullo.

HILARY (U.S.). Hullo, Pat. I say—is it true?

PATRICIA. Is what true?

HILARY. That there's been a murder.

PATRICIA. Nothing would surprise me in this place!

    (*Exit* PATRICIA, U.L.)

HILARY. Oh. (*Calling after her.*) Well—where's the body?

JENNY. I'm over here!

HILARY (*in to* R. *of sofa*). Now, look here, young lady—

JENNY (*sitting up*). If you hit me, I shall send for the police! (*Puts up her fists.*)

HILARY. I'm not going to hit you, you silly girl. And anyhow, I *am* the police. Where's the body? (*Glances around.*)

JENNY. You asked that before.

HILARY. Well, where is it, then? (*Looking behind armchair, etc.*) It must be around here *somewhere.* (*Stops looking and comes to her.*) Or am I wasting my time? There hasn't been a murder at all, has there? *Has there?*

JENNY (*in a tiny voice*). No . . .

HILARY. I *thought* so!

    (JENNY *cries noisily.*)

Well, there's nothing to cry about. Don't be silly, Jenny—look, I—Jenny! Oh, for heaven's sake! Jenny!

    (*He takes off his helmet and puts it on the floor* R. *of sofa, then sits* R. *of her.*)

(*Gently.*) Jenny—I don't *mind* that there's no body—really I don't.

JENNY (*her face changing into a broad smile*). You don't?

HILARY. No. As a matter of fact, I'm glad!

JENNY. Are you sure of that?

HILARY. Yes. I might have had to arrest someone.

JENNY. Good! And I bet you'll be even *more* glad when I tell you the reason *why* I wanted to see you.

HILARY. Well—what *was* the reason?

JENNY. I've made up my mind.

HILARY. What about?

JENNY. About you and me.

HILARY (*ominously*). And what about—you and me?

JENNY. I've decided that my answer's "yes".

HILARY. What was the *question*?

JENNY. Why—whether or not I'll marry you, of course!

HILARY. Marry me? But I haven't *asked* you yet!

JENNY (*blithely*). It's only a matter of time! You *will*!

HILARY. How do you know?

(*A pause.* JENNY *looks forlorn.*)

JENNY. Won't you?

HILARY. No! I—I've never even thought about it. And even if I *did*, it wouldn't be for hundreds and hundreds of years—and by then, I'd be a very old man—and so would you. (*As she screws up her face.*) And there's no need to cry. Oh, dear! (*Rises, to* D.R.)

JENNY. Where are you going?

HILARY. I have to see his Lordship!

JENNY. Well, you forgot your hat!

(HILARY *comes back, gets his helmet and goes* D.R. *He turns at door, but* JENNY *cries noisily again and he goes quickly.* JENNY *remains sitting on sofa.* CHESTER *enters* U.L.)

CHESTER. I say, are you all right?

JENNY (*on a loud wail*). Ye-es!

CHESTER. You don't sound it. Has something upset you?

JENNY. Ye-es!

CHESTER. I thought so. Are you unhappy?

CHESTER }
JENNY   } (*together*). Ye-es!!

CHESTER. Why don't you tell me what's the matter?

JENNY. It's rather a long story.

CHESTER. Well, give me a rough idea. (*Sits sofa,* R. *end.*)

JENNY. It's that man.

CHESTER. Which man?

JENNY. Hilary!

CHESTER. Oh, I see! And he's upset you? (*She opens her mouth to wail* "*Ye-es*".) All right, I know! What's he done?

JENNY. It isn't what he's done, it's what he *hasn't* done.

CHESTER. Oh—what he *hasn't* done? What's that?

JENNY. Say that he'll marry me.

CHESTER. Marry you? But you're a little young to think of that. aren't you?

JENNY. I'm seventeen . . .

CHESTER. Oh, seventeen! You're afraid you're going to be left on the shelf, is that it?

JENNY. I love him . . .

CHESTER. Oh, now, Jenny—

JENNY. I *do* . . .

CHESTER (*gently*). What makes you so sure?

JENNY. Have *you* never fallen in love?

CHESTER. Yes. Yes, as a matter of fact, I have.

JENNY. Long ago?

CHESTER. No—not very.

JENNY. When?

CHESTER. This morning.

JENNY. Not with—?

CHESTER. Yes.

JENNY. And she—?

CHESTER. No.

JENNY. But I thought— (CHESTER *shakes his head.*) Oh, I'm sorry.
            (*Pause. They are sitting side by side.*)

JENNY. I think she's very silly. You're not *too* bad.

CHESTER. Oh, thank you very much!

JENNY. I wonder *why* Hilary doesn't like me.

CHESTER. He probably does.

JENNY. Well, he certainly never shows it. Perhaps it's because I'm not seductive.

CHESTER (*with a smile*). Could be.

JENNY. Perhaps I ought to *try* to be.

CHESTER. Couldn't do any harm.

JENNY. How *can* I look seductive in *these* things?

CHESTER. Well, why don't you take them off?

JENNY. What?

CHESTER. And put on something more suitable.

JENNY. I might at that!
CHESTER. Why not?
JENNY (*rising*). Now?
CHESTER. No time like the present!
JENNY. Oh, thank you! You're sweet!
     (*She kisses him impulsively and runs off upstairs.* CHESTER *rises, with a smile. Then reacts as* MISS PARTRIDGE *enters through the fireplace, carrying a skull.*)
CHESTER (*below* R. *end of sofa*). Where on earth did you find that?
MISS PARTRIDGE (*below* L. *end of sofa*). In the pantry.
CHESTER. Well, you'd better put it back again. It's the cook's lucky charm. (*Moves to* D.C.)
MISS PARTRIDGE. Part of this looks most familiar.
CHESTER. Really? Which part?
MISS PARTRIDGE (*to him*). Would you care to examine it?
CHESTER. Oh. Oh—thanks. (*Takes it.*) H'm. Reminds me of somebody I know. (*Glances at her head.*)
MISS PARTRIDGE. He has a sad expression, don't you think?
CHESTER. I'm not altogether surprised! (*Bus. with lower jaw of skull.*)
MISS PARTRIDGE. Well, I mustn't dally! (*Goes towards stairs.*)
CHESTER. Oh, no! (*Follows to* U.C.) Here—you've forgotten your friend.
MISS PARTRIDGE (*at foot of stairs*). Oh, thank you. (*Takes skull.*) I'm off to my bed now.
CHESTER (*absent-mindedly*). I'll be up in a minute.
     (MISS PARTRIDGE *reacts and goes off upstairs.* ADA *enters, wearing her coat, hat and gloves, carrying her case and handbag. In to* C.)
CHESTER. What are you doing?
ADA. Going!
CHESTER. Going where?
ADA. Away from 'ere.
CHESTER. But I might need you. You're my only ally.
ADA. It's more than I can stand, sir. I've 'ad enough, and I'm going.
     (*She moves towards door* C.)
CHESTER. Ada!
          (ADA *stops, turns slowly.*)
ADA. Oh . . .
CHESTER. What's the matter?
ADA. You called me Ada.

CHESTER. That's your name, isn't it?

ADA. But you've never called me that before, sir! I didn't realize!

CHESTER. What?

ADA. That you're in *love* with me, sir!

CHESTER. What!

ADA. Oh, sir! (*Drops bag and approaches him with arms outstretched. He dodges round below armchair to* D.R. *She follows.*)

CHESTER. Ah-ha.! Ada!—er—Miss—er—You! Remember where you are! You're not at Butlin's, now, you know. (*Backing round above armchair.*)

ADA (*following*). I should 'ave known, sir. That quiver in your voice whenever I came near you—

CHESTER (L. *of telephone table*). Now, don't be silly—(*Picks up receiver.*) Give me strength! (*Hangs up and continues retreating to* C.)

ADA. That's why you shared your secrets with me—

CHESTER. Nothing of the sort!

ADA (*with closed eyes and arms outstretched*). Take me, sir! The answer's yes!

      (CHESTER *moves on tiptoe below her and makes for the door* D.R. *She opens her eyes, turns to see him escaping.*)

Ah!

CHESTER. S'sh! It's only me!

ADA (*to below armchair*). Shall I arrange with the canon, sir?

CHESTER. What about?

ADA. About the ceremony, of course.

CHESTER. Certainly not! (*Circles below her to* C.) And anyhow, the canon isn't there any more.

ADA. Why not?

CHESTER. He went off unexpectedly!

      (*Noise off from* CAPONE *and* WEDGWOOD. CHESTER *takes* ADA's *glasses and puts them on himself, turns up the collar of his jacket and stands still.* ADA *clears slightly,* D.R. CAPONE *and* WEDGWOOD *come in* U.L.)

CAPONE (*passing* CHESTER). Excuse me, sir.

      (CAPONE *and* WEDGWOOD *walk past* CHESTER *without recognizing him, to* ADA, D.R.)

CAPONE (*to* ADA). Have you seen Mr. Newton-Strangeways?

ADA. Oh—are you looking for him?

CAPONE. Yes, we are. (*He and* WEDGWOOD *look around* U.S.)

CHESTER (*to* ADA). Would you help me to sit down, dear?

ADA. What? Oh! Oh, yes, sir. (*She assists* CHESTER *as a blind man to the sofa. As he sits* R. *end he whispers.*)

CHESTER. Get the bags!

ADA. What?

CHESTER. Go and get my things!

ADA. What for?

CHESTER. We're leaving.

ADA. Who is?

CHESTER. You and me—*now!*

ADA (*delighted*). Oh, sir! (*Starts to go, then returns.*) I'd better have my glasses, sir.

CHESTER (*without thinking*). Oh, yes. (*Gives them to her.*)

(*Exit* ADA *upstairs taking case and handbag.*

CHESTER *realizes that the glasses have gone. He picks up a magazine as* CAPONE *and* WEDGWOOD *come* D.S. *to* R. *of sofa and pretends to be reading it—very close to his eyes.*

*Bus. Eventually* CAPONE'S *suspicions are aroused and he removes the magazine forcibly.*)

CAPONE. You!!

CHESTER. You see—I've been here all the time!

CAPONE. I am going to kill you, Mr. Dreadnought.

CHESTER. Oh, you wouldn't! (*Rises, round* L. *to above sofa.*)

CAPONE. Yes, I would. (*He and* WEDGWOOD *follow* CHESTER.)

CHESTER. What—now? (*Above armchair, round* R. *to below it.*)

CAPONE. Yes—now! (*Following.*)

CHESTER. Before supper? (*To* C.)

CAPONE. This minute. (*Following.*)

CHESTER. Oh, no, you won't! I have a gun! (*Produces a small gun.*)

CAPONE. *I* have a bigger one. (*Produces big gun.*)

CHESTER. So you have.

CAPONE. *Mine* is loaded.

CHESTER. So is mine! (*He squirts his water pistol in* CAPONE'S *face and runs off* L., *pursued by* CAPONE *and* WEDGWOOD.)

(*After a moment* HILARY *enters* D.R., *looking around cautiously for* JENNY. *Telephone bell. He answers it.*)

HILARY. Hullo . . . Who? The Police Station? Oh—Who do you want? . . . P.C. Pond? Just a moment, I'll see if he's in. (*Starts to go* U.L., *reacts.*) Oh—Pond speaking . . . Yes, sir . . . No, sir

. . . Yes, sir . . . No, sir . . . Yes, sir . . . No, sir . . . Oh,
sir! . . . Very good, sir! (*Hangs up with a sigh.*)
    (JENNY *appears at the top of the stairs. She is dressed in a clinging
evening dress, and has her hair newly done in a sophisticated way. She
is smoking a cigarette in an immensely long holder.*)
JENNY (*in a pseudo-seductive voice*). Good evening . . .
HILARY (*turns to glance at her, looks away, reacts, and looks at her again.*)
Oh, no! (*He turns away* R., *painfully, and sinks his face into his hand.*)
    (JENNY *wanders down* C., *swaying seductively, and settles herself
on the sofa,* L. *end. She sighs and exhales a cloud of smoke.*)
JENNY. Why don't you come and sit down here—
HILARY. Look, Jenny, I—
JENNY. —next to me?
    (*She pats the sofa next to her, and gazes at him enigmatically.
Reluctantly he moves to the sofa and sits, but at the* R. *end, away from
her. He gazes out front impassively. She lies back and looks even more
seductive. She sighs loudly.*)
Do you notice anything different about me?
    (HILARY *turns, looks her over and faces front again.*)
HILARY (*firmly*). No.
JENNY. I've changed!
HILARY. Oh, so you have! Do you think you *ought* to come down
here in your nightdress?
JENNY (*dropping her assumed voice and lapsing back into Scots*). This is
*not* my nightdress!
HILARY. Isn't it? Oh, I'm sorry.
    (*She resumes her poise after a second. She rises and crosses below
him, swaying her hips rather obviously. She goes to door* U.L. *and
switches off the main lighting. He reacts. She returns the way she went,
swaying and sighing, and sits sofa again. Suddenly she lies full-length
on the sofa with her head in his lap. She blows smoke up into his face.
He splutters and she smiles delightedly.*)
JENNY. If you really *wanted* to . . . you could call me—darling!
HILARY. That's awfully decent of you!
JENNY. What can *I* call you?
HILARY. What's wrong with Hilary?
JENNY. Oh, nothing—but isn't there something more . . . intimate
—that I can call you when we're alone?
HILARY. No, I don't think there is.

JENNY. Haven't you got a nickname? (*Gleefully, sitting up L. of him as he reacts.*) You have!

HILARY (*trying to rise*). I think I'd better be going— (*She restrains him.*)

JENNY. Tell me your nickname first—

HILARY. No, really—there are some things one just doesn't—

JENNY. It'll be our little secret—

HILARY. No!—I refuse—emphatically—I *couldn't*—

JENNY. I won't let you go until you do!

(*Pause. Bus. of making up mind.*)

HILARY. Oh, very well! It was at school, you see. I—(*Rising.*) Oh, no, I can't!

JENNY (*rising also*). Come on!

HILARY. But it sounds so silly—

JENNY. Well?

HILARY (*painfully*). It happened during a Nature Study ramble.

JENNY. Yes?

HILARY. I was the first boy they'd ever had there called Pond. So—so they used to call me Lily.

JENNY. Lily Pond!

HILARY. Now you're laughing at me.

JENNY. Well, I— (*She stops suddenly.*) Would you take this cigarette, please?

(*He takes it and puts it out at table L. She is standing very still, beginning to look a little green. He comes to her.*)

HILARY. What's the matter?

JENNY (*plaintively*). I . . . I think I'm going . . . to be sick . . .!

HILARY. Oh, no! Where's the bathroom?

(*He looks around in panic, then picks her up in a fireman's lift and carries her off upstairs.*

*As they go, CHESTER re-appears from L. and sees them. He switches lights on. He looks around for a sign of the crooks, then moves to R.C.*

*ADA enters with his camera and bag from upstairs.*)

CHESTER. What are you doing with my camera? And my bag, too!

'ADA. You sent me for them, sir. (*Puts camera and bag U.S.*)

CHESTER. I did?

ADA. Yes. Don't you remember—you said we were going away together!

CHESTER (*ruefully*). Oh, yes, so I did.

ADA (*coming down level*). And this—this is mine! (*Produces a tiny week-end case.*)

(CHESTER *looks at it for a moment.*)

CHESTER. Are you going for long?

ADA (*gazing at him*). Long enough, sir!

CHESTER. Ah-ha! That's enough!

ADA. Shall we go, now, then, sir?

CHESTER (*playing for time*). Well, all right—but there's something I must do before we go.

ADA. What's that, sir?

CHESTER. Er—I'll tell you when I've done it! (*Going to door* U.L.) I won't be long.

ADA. I'll wait here, sir.

CHESTER. Yes, you do that. (*Dramatically.*) And don't worry—I shall be back—very soon!

(*He goes out, but re-enters immediately, unconscious, carried by* CAPONE *and* WEDGWOOD, *who put him on sofa.* WEDGWOOD L. *of sofa,* CAPONE R.)

CAPONE (*to* ADA). Mr. Dreadnought is temporarily indisposed. He wants you to wait for him in the garden. (ADA *hesitates.*) *In the garden!!* (ADA *goes out* C.)

(CAPONE *tries to wake* CHESTER. *He looks around, gets the soda syphon and is about to use it.*)

CHESTER. Ah-ah! I'm awake!

CAPONE. You didn't really think you would get away from us, did you?

CHESTER. No, not really. I was only pretending.

CAPONE. The time is up, Mr. Dreadnought.

CHESTER (*looks at his watch*). So it is!

CAPONE. The photograph—if you please.

CHESTER. I—I couldn't find it.

CAPONE (*seeing bag* U.S.). Then we shall have to find it for you. (*Goes to bag.* WEDGWOOD *joins him, on his* R.)

CHESTER. Oh, *would* you? You are kind!

(CAPONE *and* WEDGWOOD *tip out the contents of* CHESTER'S *bag and find the photograph.*)

CAPONE. This is it.

CHESTER (*to* L. *of* CAPONE). Oh, *that* one! What a pity you were pulling such a face!

CAPONE. Perhaps it would be a good idea to burn the contents—just in case you still have the negative. Maybe an even better idea would be to destroy *you*, also.

CHESTER. I shall scream for help!

CAPONE. We don't need any help.

(*During the next speech,* HILARY *comes downstairs.* CAPONE *and* WEDGWOOD *see him, but* CHESTER, *his back to the stairs, does not.*)

CHESTER (*tentatively brave*). If you think you can scare me you're mistaken. I'm not afraid of you. You come here like a couple of broker's men and think you can frighten *me!* Give me that picture! (*To his surprise,* CAPONE *hands back the photograph, having seen the Arm of the Law at the foot of the stairs.*) Good! That's better! Now, you just get out of here. You hear me? Go on—clear out!

(CAPONE *and* WEDGWOOD *turn and go quickly off* D.R. CHESTER *is amazed, smiles, dusts his hands, turns and sees* HILARY.)

CHESTER. I say!

HILARY. What?

CHESTER. Do you want to make an arrest?

HILARY. Why, what have you done?

CHESTER. Not me! —Somebody else!

HILARY. Well, I don't know—

CHESTER. There are two people in this place who are going to kill me.

HILARY (*brightening*). Oh—then there's been no actual *crime*, yet?

CHESTER. Well, no—

HILARY. Good show! Come back and tell me when the crime's been committed.

CHESTER. Oh, very well. (*Moves away,* R. *slightly, then returns.*) I shan't be able to!

HILARY. Oh, no, of course not. I am foolhardy! Well, never mind— I shall get to know about it.

CHESTER (*thrusting the photograph at him*). Look at this!

HILARY. H'm—jolly good!

CHESTER. Don't you recognize anybody?

HILARY. Well, I . . . By jove, yes! Those two chaps in the background. Aren't they the piano-tuning chaps?

CHESTER. They are! You see what they're doing?

HILARY. Coming out of a jeweller's shop.

CHESTER. Exactly! Those two men have just held up and robbed that shop!

HILARY (*pained*). Oh, no!

CHESTER. Oh, yes! And if I don't give them back this picture they're going to kill me. What do you think I should do?

HILARY. I should give it back! (*Hands back the photo and moves away below sofa.*)

CHESTER. What are you going to do about it?

HILARY. Me?

CHESTER. Yes—you!

HILARY. I say, you're not suggesting I should arrest them, are you?

CHESTER. Why not?

HILARY. I have a certain reputation in the Force.

CHESTER. You have?

HILARY. Oh, yes. Never arrested anyone *yet*.

CHESTER. No?

HILARY. Most emphatically, no! If I did, I shouldn't be able to raise my head again. I'd never live it down.

> (*Enter* PATRICIA *from upstairs. She is very angry. She comes down* C. CHESTER *is* R.C., HILARY *below sofa.*)

PATRICIA. Mr. Dreadnought!

CHESTER. What's the matter?

PATRICIA. Are you going to hand it over now, or shall I call the police?

CHESTER. Now, don't *you* start! (*Away* D.S. *slightly.*)

PATRICIA (*advancing, eyes blazing*). I want to speak to you alone for a moment?

CHESTER. Ah! I'm afraid that's impossible. (*Crosses to* R. *of* HILARY.)

PATRICIA. Why?

CHESTER. Because this is my lawyer—Mr. Winch.

PATRICIA. Mr. Winch?

CHESTER. Yes. Of Winch, Pinch, Clinch and Blunt.

HILARY. Who's Blunt?

CHESTER. The office boy.

HILARY. I thought his name was Sharpe.

CHESTER. Oh, that was *years* ago! Don't you remember . . .?

PATRICIA. Chester!!

CHESTER. Yes, dear?

PATRICIA. I said I wished to speak to you.

CHESTER. So you did.

PATRICIA. I was a fool ever to be taken in by you in the first place.

CHESTER. What do you mean?

PATRICIA. Forcing your way in here under false pretences, and expecting us to believe a string of ridiculous lies! And now this!

CHESTER. Do you mind telling me what you're talking about?

PATRICIA. I am talking about my mother's pearl necklace, which was there this morning—and is now missing!

CHESTER. But you can't seriously think that I—

PATRICIA. And it's no good trying to talk your way out of it this time—

CHESTER. But, darling—!

PATRICIA. Don't you "darling" me! I hate you! Do you hear? I hate you! (*He starts to go to door* C.) Where are you going?

CHESTER. South Africa.

PATRICIA (*amidst tears*). South Africa's *that* way!

CHESTER. I'm so sorry. (*Moves below* PATRICIA *to* D.R.)

PATRICIA. I know you now for what you are!

CHESTER. What am I?

PATRICIA (*to below armchair*). A scheming blackguard with no more decency than a—toad!

CHESTER. Don't call me a toad!

PATRICIA. You snake!

CHESTER. That's better.

PATRICIA (*to* HILARY). Why do you just *stand* there? Why don't you telephone the police?

HILARY. Oh, yes. Of course. (*At phone.*) Give me the police . . . Hullo, this is Elrood Castle. We want the police right away . . . What? . . . Really? . . . Oh. (*Hangs up.*) He says they're already here. (*Sees his own uniform.*) Oh! I am impossible! (*Exit upstairs.*)
            (PATRICIA *moves* C. CHESTER *follows and stops her by the arm.*)

CHESTER. Won't you let me explain?

PATRICIA. It's no good. I shall never believe another word you say.

CHESTER (*thrusting the photograph at her*). Look at this!

PATRICIA (*without looking*). What?

CHESTER. This photograph in the hands of the police would get your piano tuners arrested in two minutes.

PATRICIA (*to below* L. *end of sofa*). Then why don't you hand it over to Hilary?

CHESTER (*to* R. *of her*). I tried! But he wasn't interested.
            (*Enter* CAPONE *and* WEDGWOOD *from* D.R.)

PATRICIA (*to* C.). Ah! You're just in time, Mr. Capone.

CAPONE (*puzzled*). We are?

PATRICIA. Yes. This—*person*—has just robbed my mother.

CAPONE. Indeed!

PATRICIA. I would be glad if you would keep an eye on him until the police arrive.

CHESTER. But you can't—!

CAPONE. We would be delighted. (*They move in to either side of* CHESTER, CAPONE R., WEDGWOOD L.)

CHESTER. Don't you dare come near me!

CAPONE. Why? What will you do?

CHESTER. I'll think of something. (CAPONE *grabs his arm.*)

CAPONE. Come, Wedgwood. (*No reaction.*) Wedgwood!

CHESTER (*to* WEDGWOOD). Oh, do pay attention!

CAPONE. Perhaps I had better relieve you of *this* first. (*He tries to take photograph.*)

CHESTER. That's all right—it isn't very heavy!

CAPONE. Give it to me!

CHESTER. Ah-ha! No, you don't! (*Breaks free, to* L. *of* PATRICIA.) Pat, the least you can do is to take this picture and keep it safe. You must believe me—it's terribly important! (*Pushes it into her hands.*) Give it to Hilary.

(CAPONE *and* WEDGWOOD *grab him again and pull him away* D.L. *Telephone bell.* PATRICIA *answers it.*)

PATRICIA (*into phone*). Hullo . . . Yes, this is Elrood Castle. . . . Oh, hullo, Sergeant MacIntyre . . . What? . . . Descriptions of which men? (CAPONE *and* WEDGWOOD *react.*) Oh, I see. All right, I'll just jot them down. (*She gets a pencil.* CAPONE *and* WEDGWOOD *hold* CHESTER *as he tries to move.*) Yes, I've got that . . . Yes . . . Yes . . . Good. All right, Sergeant, we'll keep our eyes open for them. (*Hangs up.*) They're circulating the descriptions of the two men who held up that jeweller's shop last week.

CAPONE. Is that so? What—are the descriptions?

PATRICIA (*reads*). One short, thick-set, wearing a loud suit and a bright tie. And the other—tall, about six foot—dressed in black—(*Looks at* CAPONE. *As she realizes, her voice peters out.*)—pale face . . . dark eyes . . .

(CHESTER *raises his eyes to heaven.* CAPONE *is ominously still.* Even WEDGWOOD *has sensed the atmosphere and has stopped chewing.*)

CAPONE (*moving towards her*). Have you seen anyone bearing those descriptions?

PATRICIA. Why—why, no! —no, of course not . . .

CHESTER. Are you sure?

CAPONE. Had it not occurred to you that those descriptions might easily fit Mr. Wedgwood and myself?

PATRICIA (*edging U.C. towards stairs as* CAPONE *circles round to her R.*). You two? Good heavens, no! Not in the least! Nothing like you—nothing at all!

CAPONE. Please give me that picture.
(PATRICIA *turns and rushes off upstairs.*)
(*To* WEDGWOOD.) Don't let him out of your sight!
(*He rushes off after* PATRICIA. *Exit.*
WEDGWOOD *takes out a gun and covers* CHESTER.)

CHESTER. Seasonal weather for the time of the year!
(*Enter* LORD ELROOD, *from D.R. with his shotgun.*)

ELROOD. Huh! Prisoner, eh? Who is he? Good heavens! It's the General! (*Comes to attention, salutes.*) What are you doing to him, eh? What are you doing? I see! (*He abruptly raises his gun and digs it in* WEDGWOOD'S *stomach. He takes* WEDGWOOD'S *gun.* WEDGWOOD *backs L.* ELROOD *crosses* CHESTER.)

CHESTER. Well done! You were just in time!

ELROOD Why didn't you give the alarm?

CHESTER. It was all so sudden.

ELROOD. Yes. I can see that. Who's this feller?

CHESTER. Oh—this is Mr. Wedgwood.

ELROOD. Wedgwood?

CHESTER. Yes. He's an old China of mine! As a matter of fact—
(*Whispers to* LORD ELROOD.)

ELROOD. What? (*To* WEDGWOOD.) So I've got you at last, have I? (*Advances on* WEDGWOOD.) So *you're* the feller! Got rid of your uniform, I see. I've waited a long time to get to grips with you! (*He advances and pursues* WEDGWOOD *above sofa, down C and off D.R., shouting ad lib.*)
(CHESTER *watches them go, highly amused.* JENNY *comes downstairs, carrying her volume of Shakespeare.*)

JENNY. What was Lord Elrood shouting about?

CHESTER (*to her at C.*). I've made his day.

JENNY. How?

CHESTER. I told him that Mr. Wedgwood is the postman!

JENNY. Oh, I see. By the way, did you know that you've got competition?

CHESTER. What do you mean?

JENNY. Well, Mr. Capone's chasing Pat all over the top floor!

CHESTER. Pat! Oh, my God!

(*He brushes her aside and rushes off upstairs. She shrugs, then stretches out on the sofa and reads aloud from her book. Throughout the following chase she continues reading, oblivious of what is going on around her.*)

JENNY   " 'tis but thy name that is my enemy;—

Thou art thyself though, not a Montague.

What's Montague? It is nor hand, nor foot,

Nor arm, nor face, nor any other part

Belonging to a man.˙ O! Be some other name! . . ."

(*She continues reading.*

*There is a loud report off* D.R., *then* WEDGWOOD *rushes on from cellar* D.R. *pursued by* LORD ELROOD. *They go off* U.L.

CHESTER *comes downstairs, followed by* CAPONE. *They go off into the cellar* D.R.

HILARY *comes downstairs, holding the photograph, and goes off* U.L.

CHESTER *re-appears from* D.R. *He takes the shade from the standard lamp and puts it over his head, remaining standing near the lamp.*

WEDGWOOD *from* U.L. *Passes* CHESTER, *turns back and pulls* CHESTER'S *tie. The standard lamp goes on. He pulls the tie again. The lamp goes off again.* LORD ELROOD *runs on from* U.L. *and pursues* WEDGWOOD *off* D.R.

CHESTER *removes the shade from his head, replaces it on the standard lamp and moves* D.C.

HILARY *comes in from* U.L. *still studying the photograph.*)

HILARY. Where are they?

CHESTER. Down there!

(HILARY *moves back towards door* U.L.)

No, you don't! (*He pushes* HILARY *down the cellar steps, and follows him.*)

(LADY ELROOD *and* PATRICIA *come downstairs, to* C.)

LADY ELROOD. Why aren't there swarms of anxious constables rushing in and out of the keep? I don't know what they think we pay them for!

PATRICIA. I wonder where he is . . .

LADY ELROOD. Who?

PATRICIA. Chester—I must find him—
           (*Enter* CHESTER *from* D.R.)

CHESTER. You have. This is a great day for the police force.

LADY ELROOD. Why?

CHESTER. Hilary has just made two arrests!

LADY ELROOD. What?

JENNY (*jumping up from the sofa*). It isn't true! It can't be true!

CHESTER. I'm afraid it *is*—

JENNY. But he'll be so unhappy! I must go to him! I must go to him at once! (*She rushes off* D.R.)
           (CHESTER *produces the necklace.*)

CHESTER. I've got something for you, Lady Elrood. (*Gives it to her.*)

LADY ELROOD. My necklace! You found it!

CHESTER. Yes—in Mr. Wedgwood's pocket!

LADY ELROOD (*taking it*). Oh, I'm so grateful! Do you know, Pat thought it—

CHESTER. Yes. I *know* what Pat thought.
           (PATRICIA *to below sofa.*)

LADY ELROOD (*moving to stairs*). Well, I must go and put this somewhere safe. (*Turns.*) I told her you couldn't possibly be as dishonest as you looked! (*Exit upstairs.*)
           (CHESTER *moves to* R. *of* PATRICIA.
     *Enter from* D.R., CAPONE, WEDGWOOD *and* HILARY *in a line, handcuffed to each other.* HILARY *stops in the doorway disconsolately.*)

HILARY. Oh, I shall never live this down—never, as long as I live . . .
           (*They all move in single file up to the door* C., *and we now see that* JENNY *is handcuffed to* HILARY'S R. *wrist, and is smiling up at him delightedly. They all go out* C.
     *There is a pause.* CHESTER *and* PATRICIA *look at each other.*)

PATRICIA. I'm sorry I was so stupid . . .

CHESTER (*gently*). You weren't stupid.
           (*They move gradually nearer to each other.*)
Tell me—what's he like?

PATRICIA. Who?

CHESTER. Your boy friend.

PATRICIA. Boy friend?

CHESTER. The one you said you were in love with.

PATRICIA (*with a smile*). I told that to Mrs. Gribble. You weren't supposed to hear.

CHESTER. Well, as a matter of fact—Mrs. Gribble . . . was me.

PATRICIA. I know.

CHESTER. You know?

PATRICIA. Yes. Of course. Why else did you think I said that about loving someone else?

CHESTER. You mean— . . . There's no-one?

PATRICIA. Well, there *wasn't* . . . until now . . .

CHESTER. And now?

PATRICIA. Now I rather think there is . . .

(*They are about to kiss. There is a loud report from off* D.R.)

ELROOD (*off* D.R.). Marcellus! Help! Help! Marcellus!

*He rushes in from* D.R., *thoroughly distraught. He no longer carries his shotgun. He runs across and off upstairs, calling frantically the whole time.*

*From* D.R. *comes the determined, uniformed figure of the* POSTMAN. *He carries* LORD ELROOD's *shotgun at the ready, and there is a grim look in his eye. He walks slowly and purposefully towards the stairs as—*

THE CURTAIN FALLS.

Printed and bound in Great Britain by
Hobbs the Printers Ltd, Totton, Hampshire

# PRODUCTION NOTE

WILD GOOSE CHASE is a farce, and as such it is essential that it be played with sincerity. A farce actor or actress must genuinely *believe* in the comic situations, or he or she will never be funny. There must be no conscious attempt to be amusing. Chester Dreadnought really believes that Capone and Wedgwood are going to kill him. He must be sincerely desperate, and his attempts to evade them and conceal himself (even in a suit of armour!) must be genuine, and will then be amusing to the audience.

Though Chester is obviously the leading rôle, this is a play which depends for its success on the team-work of the entire company.

The play starts off literally with a "bang", but the bulk of Act One is more light comedy than actual farce, and it does not become really broad until Act Two. All the most farcical things in the play are in this Act, and it is therefore essential that the Third Act be played at a good pace and with terrific drive, building up to the final curtain.

Quite apart from requiring an inexhaustible supply of physical energy, Chester Dreadnought must be played with great charm as well as with impeccable timing and the sincerity already referred to. All these qualities were notable in the performances of Mr. Leslie Phillips, who played the part in the Embassy production, and Mr. Frederick Jaeger, who played in the original production at the New Theatre, Hull.

Lord Elrood is a man living in an imaginary world of his own, and he must never for a moment step out of this world. If he does, even for a moment, the comedy of the character will be lost. Lady Elrood is easy-going, well-dressed, and has a dry humour—as she was portrayed so delightfully by Miss Joan Haythorne at the Embassy

The two crooks, Capone and Wedgwood, are two of the most important parts in the play. They are an integral part of nearly all Chester's comedy. They are the pivot around which he revolves. Capone must be as tall and darkly menacing as possible, and should be played with a hard German accent. Wedgwood should have an expressionless face, and a dog-like devotion to Capone. He should follow his superior like a shadow, and his slow gum-chewing can be almost as menacing as Capone's more obvious threats.

Miss Partridge is an eccentric, and is probably the most broadly characterized part in the play. She should be intense, voluble—and sincere. Miss Joan Sanderson was ideally cast, and was outstanding in the London production.

Hilary Pond should be played as a very "Public School" type of policeman. His pained resignation when he is eventually forced to make an arrest, and his earlier attempts to avoid doing so, are highly entertaining. If it is possible for the actor to be tall and thin, so much the better, as he and the love-sick Scots teenager, Jenny Stewart, then make an ill-assorted and amusing couple. Patricia's main function is to look lovely, wear pretty clothes, and be a charming and attractive partner to the leading man. This does not mean that it is a dull character—it must *not* be.

Ada, the cockney maid, should nearly always remain rather shy, gauche and awestruck. Her outbursts, to Lady Elrood in Act Two (page 35) and to Chester in Act Three (page 66), are then more surprising and more effective.

In the scene between Patricia and Chester (as "Mrs. Gribble") in Act Two (page 52), it must be clear to the audience that she realizes that "Mrs. Gribble" is really Chester, so that they can enjoy the situation of her deliberately provoking him about his appearance, etc. The moment after Patricia says "I'm already in love with somebody else" (page 53) must be played for complete pathos. We must feel really sorry for Chester as he moves sadly away on "Oh. I see . . ." A moment like this can be most effective in the middle of a farce, but the minute it is over—with the entrance of Capone and Wedgwood—the pace must be picked up and increased rapidly to the moment when the curtain falls on Act Two.

There are two "chase" sequences in the play, one in Act Two and one in Act Three. In both cases, they must be played at terrific speed. There must be no lull in the middle of them, and so the various individual crosses must overlap ever so slightly.

In the "seduction" scene between Jenny and Hilary in Act Three (page 68), it is advisable for Jenny to abandon her Scots accent and assume a low, seductive drawl. Her transformation must be staggering. Her evening dress should be clinging and super-sophisticated, her hair should be piled high on her head, she should wear long earrings and smoke a cigarette in an immensely long holder.

The "cigarette business" referred to in Act Two (page 55) is quite easy if these directions are followed:—

1. Capone takes out cigarette as Wedgwood gets out matches;
2. Chester takes cigarette from Capone's right hand as Capone searches for lighter, and Wedgwood strikes a match;
3. Chester goes to light cigarette at Wedgwood's match, but Capone takes back the cigarette and lights his lighter;
4. Chester blows out lighter. The match burns Wedgwood's fingers;
5. Capone rises to fireplace. Chester blows on Wedgwood's fingers to cool them;
6. Wedgwood rises and doffs his hat in thanks;
7. Chester rises and doffs his hat also, but his wig comes with it and they recognize him.

It is helpful if Chester's hat is sewn on to his wig, both for this business and for when he puts his hat and wig on to Miss Partridge.

At the close of the play it is essential that the Postman should move *slowly* and purposefully across the stage towards the stairs. He must not, on any account, rush it. The uniform and mail bag must leave no possible doubt as to his identity! Incidentally, the character of the Postman should *not* appear in the programme, as this will spoil the surprise value of the final curtain.

DEREK BENFIELD

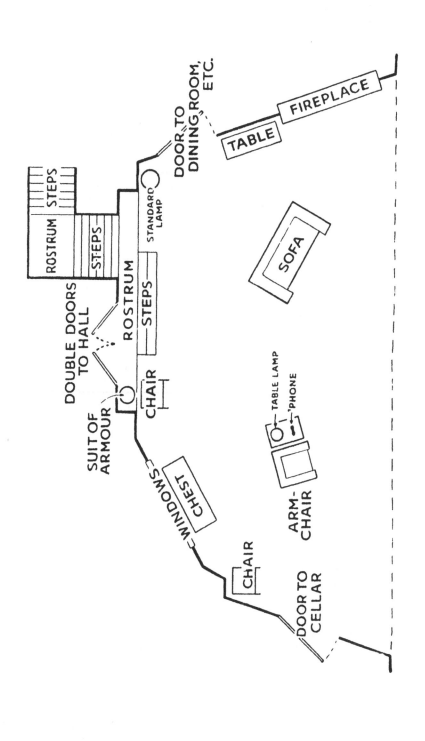

# PROPERTY PLOT

## ACT ONE

**SET**

Magazines (chest).
Letters (table R.).
Telephone (table R.).
Cigarettes (mantelpiece).
Matches (mantelpiece).
Vase (table L.)
Case (ADA. Off R.).
Shotgun (LORD E. Off D.R.).
Flowers (PAT. Off D.R.).
Volume of Shakespeare (JENNY. Off L.).
Hammer (MISS P. Off R.).
Magnifying glass (MISS P. Off R.).
Handbag (MISS P. Off R.)
Various packages (MISS P. Off R.).
Camera on tripod (CHESTER. Off R.).
Suitcases containing photographs, negatives, etc. (CHESTER. Off R.).
Telegram (ADA. Off R.).

**PERSONAL**

Glasses (ADA).
Trilby hat (CHESTER).
Note-book (CHESTER).
Pencil (CHESTER).
Handkerchief (CHESTER).
Chewing gum (WEDGWOOD).

## ACT TWO

**SET**

Duster (ADA. Off L.).
Stone (MISS P. Off L.).
Telegram (PAT. Off L.).
Shakespeare (JENNY. Off L.).
Magazine (PAT. Table R.).
Tea trolley (ADA. Off L.).
Tea pot (on tea trolley).
Sugar basin with lumped sugar (on tea trolley).
Milk jug (on tea trolley).
4 cups and saucers (tea trolley).
4 side plates (tea trolley).
Cake (tea trolley).
Cake fork (tea trolley).
Soda syphon (CHESTER. Table L.)
Goose (HILARY. Off R.).

**PERSONAL**

Automatic pistol (CAPONE).
Wristlet watch (CAPONE).
Handbag (CHESTER).
Ladies' gloves (CHESTER).
Cigarettes and lighter (CAPONE).
Matches (WEDGWOOD).

## ACT THREE

**SET**

Magazine (CHESTER. Sofa).
Skull (MISS P. Off L.).
Small case (ADA. Off L.).
Ashtray (Table R.).
Camera and tripod (ADA. Off L.).
CHESTER'S case (ADA. Off L.).
Note pad (PAT. Table R.).
Pencil (PAT. Table R.).
Shakespeare (JENNY. Off L.).
Three pairs of handcuffs (Off R.).

**PERSONAL**

Cigarettes (CHESTER).
Lighter (CAPONE).
Photographs (CHESTER).
Small practical water pistol (CHESTER).
Long cigarette holder (JENNY).
Cigarette (JENNY).
Wristlet watch (CHESTER).
Necklace (CHESTER).

# COSTUME PLOT

**CHESTER**
Sports suit throughout.
Woman's tweed costume, felt hat, brogues, and red wig. (Act II).

**LADY ELROOD**
Cotton house-coat. (Act I).
Summer dress. (Act I).
Afternoon dress. (Acts II and III).

**LORD ELROOD**
Riding boots, tweed jacket, waistcoat and silk scarf.

**PATRICIA**
Cotton dress. (Acts I and II).
Evening blouse and skirt. (Act III).

**MISS PARTRIDGE**
Ill-fitting silk costume, velvet head band, beads, etc.

**JENNY**
Bright slacks, American-style shirt. (Acts I, II and III).
Sophisticated evening dress. (Act III).
Dressing-gown and slippers. (Act III).

**HILARY**
Policeman's uniform.

**ADA**
Raincoat and hat. (Act I).
Maid's uniform. (Acts I, II and III).
Gloves and handbag. (Act III).

**CAPONE**
Black suit, black shirt and tie, black shoes, black gloves.

**WEDGWOOD**
Loud check suit, bright tie, soft hat.

## LIGHTING CUES

ACT ONE:     No cues.
ACT TWO:     No cues.
ACT THREE:   At rise—table lamp only.
            Cue 1: PAT switches main lights on. (Page 57).
            Cue 2: JENNY turns main lighting off. (Page 68).
            Cue 3: CHESTER turns main lighting on. (Page 69).
            Cue 4: Practical standard lamp on. (Page 76).
            Cue 5: Practical standard lamp off. (Page 76).

## EFFECTS

**ACT ONE**
3 gun shots.
Door-bell.

**ACT TWO**
2 gun shots.
Armour falling down stone steps.
Trumpet alarm.

**ACT THREE**
2 gun shots.
Telephone bell.

## MUSIC

"Post Horn Gallop" before the curtain rises on each Act.

## MUSIC USE NOTE

Licensees are solely responsible for obtaining formal written permission from copyright owners to use copyrighted music in the performance of this play and are strongly cautioned to do so. If no such permission is obtained by the licensee, then the licensee must use only original music that the licensee owns and controls. Licensees are solely responsible and liable for all music clearances and shall indemnify the copyright owners of the play(s) and their licensing agent, Samuel French, against any costs, expenses, losses and liabilities arising from the use of music by licensees. Please contact the appropriate music licensing authority in your territory for the rights to any incidental music.

## IMPORTANT BILLING AND CREDIT REQUIREMENTS

If you have obtained performance rights to this title, please refer to your licensing agreement for important billing and credit requirements.

Lightning Source UK Ltd.
Milton Keynes UK
UKOW06f0209080515

251124UK00007B/109/P